MESSY *Beautiful* FRIENDSHIP

FINDING AND NURTURING DEEP AND LASTING RELATIONSHIPS

CHRISTINE HOOVER

BakerBooks

a division of Baker Publishing Group
Grand Rapids, Michigan

Published by Baker Books
a division of Baker Publishing Group
P.O. Box 6287, Grand Rapids, MI 49516-6287
www.bakerbooks.com

Printed in the United States of America

Library of Congress Cataloging-in-Publication Data
Names: Hoover, Christine, author.
Title: Messy beautiful friendship : finding and nurturing deep and lasting
    relationships / Christine Hoover.
Description: Grand Rapids : Baker Books, 2017. | Includes bibliographical
    references.
Identifiers: LCCN 2016046728 | ISBN 9780801019371 (pbk.)
Subjects: LCSH: Christian women—Religious life. | Female friendship—Religious
    aspects—Christianity.
Classification: LCC BV4527 .H6635 2017 | DDC 241/.6762082—dc23
LC record available at https://lccn.loc.gov/2016046728

The author is represented by the literary agency of Wolgemuth & Associates, Inc.

18   19   20   21   22   23   8   7   6   5   4

To Claire
I look forward to the day
when I get to see you again.

Contents

Introduction

This One's for the Strugglers

*M*any women privately wrestle with the complexities of adult friendship. Perhaps you are one of them.

I certainly have struggled with friendship over the years. I've known years of friendship drought. I've experienced conflicts in relationships—some of my own making—that have tied my insides in knots. I've received wounds so bitter that I've retreated to cocoon myself in the false security of isolation.

But I've also experienced deep relationships with other women that have enriched my life beyond measure, pointed me toward Christ, and challenged me to grow. These relationships have taught me that friendship is worth any struggle it takes to discover and deepen.

No matter where your friendships currently are, you've probably found that your heart never ceases longing for fulfilling companionship. Friendship seems such a rarity to find and such a fragile joy when we've found it, doesn't it?

As I've let slip that I've been writing a book on friendship, the response has been something akin to thirst. Some, in larger audiences, have audibly squealed, not because they anticipate reading my words but because they are bursting with need for relief from their private fears

9

and struggles. In one small group setting, a woman practically jumped across the table at me, reaching, as it were, for help. She is one of many seeking an oasis in a desert.

We want friends, all of us do, and not just any friends. We want relationships in which we know and are known at the deepest level. We want friendships that point us to grace and truth.

Curiously, however, we seem to be standing beside one another, holding identical longings yet resolutely believing we're alone in them. But the truth is we aren't actually wandering alone and aimless in a desert; we're practically tripping over each other as we grasp at our ideal dreams for friendship.

I've wondered at this. If we're alike in our desires, what keeps us from turning to our left and to our right to cultivate friendship with those around us?

Well, it's not that simple, you might say, as you point to your failed attempts, your open wounds, the boxes you've just unpacked in a new community, your insecurities and assumptions, or your overextended schedule.

Oh yes, I know all the reasons why it's not so simple because I've given them myself, and I know all too well how quick we are to make those reasons into excuses and those excuses into thick walls. My wall has historically been built upon the excuse that I'm a pastor's wife and women treat me differently because of it. I've rehearsed this excuse in my mind—while simultaneously taking the do-nothing, hope-for-the-best approach to friendship.

I have come to believe that our own excuses are one of our biggest obstacles to friendship, but I think there is one greater: we don't have an understanding of what true friendship is or how God designed it. In the void, we've taken up a cultural definition that makes friendship unattainably idyllic and about self: Who is doing what for *me*? How do other people make *me* feel? Who is reaching out to *me* or including *me*? Who is honoring *me*?

Without a biblical understanding of friendship, we tend toward believing we're unique and that everyone else must mold themselves around our personalities, our needs, and our schedules. As a result, we continually aspire to ideal friendship that is easy, comfortable, fun—and initiated by others. Perhaps this explains why we perpetually thirst in a desert.

As Christians, we must look to the Bible to inform our friendships. In this book you hold in your hands, we will look together to God, in his Word, for our definition and practice of friendship.

Spoiler alert: we'll find that friendship is a by-product of being more concerned with others than ourselves.

Hopefully you've picked up this book because you want deep friendships and you're done with the excuses you've erected into walls of isolation. Perhaps you've been frustrated, discouraged, or disappointed by the realities of friendship and you need some help reengaging broken relationships or fostering new ones.

Good.

You're who I wrote this book for—Christian women who need a fresh perspective on friendship, who need to know they're not alone in the wrestling, and who want to know how to navigate relationships in a way that honors God. Together, we'll shatter idealistic and unattainable dreams of friendship, embrace God-designed friendship, name threats to godly friendship, discover the means we have at our disposal to find and deepen friendship, learn what it takes to be a good friend, and learn how to receive the friendship of others.

I pray you'll find what I have discovered in my own life: friendship is messy, but even in its messiness it is beautiful indeed.

PART ONE

A New Vision for Friendship

ONE

When Did Friendship Become Such a Struggle?

It is not simply to be taken for granted that the Christian has the privilege of living among other Christians.

Dietrich Bonhoeffer[1]

When we were children, friendship merely happened to us. Friends came as easily as the sunrise and as effortlessly as the line on the doorframe by which we measured ourselves inched taller every year.

We didn't have to think about making friends. We simply approached the monkey bars on the playground, signed up for an after-school team, or steered our bikes onto the neighborhood sidewalks, and, within seconds, we were swept up in a swarm of similarly aged kids barreling toward the ice cream truck blaring circus music on loop. We were racing alongside our teammates to the concession stand for after-game snow cones or migrating together through the neighborhood in gangs of three-wheelers, scooters, and Schwinns.

Our mothers, when probing for the day's details, referred to this random assortment of kids as our "friends." And we supposed they actually were, because they generally liked what we liked, lived where we lived, and did what we did. They were in our proximity, moving in the same kid orbit; therefore, they were our friends.

My grade-school best friend lived around the corner from me in a house that smelled of stale cigarettes. On sticky summer days, we'd lie on our stomachs on her brown-and-white speckled shag carpet, chins propped on our fists and feet thrust in the air, watching people get slimed on Nickelodeon, a channel I didn't get at home. She had a white canopy bed with high posters, which we'd use as microphones to belt out Whitney Houston songs as we jumped around on her bedspread. Famished from these rock star demands, we'd run to the kitchen for Oatmeal Creme Pies, and afterward she'd teach me ballet positions using the oven handle as our barre.

We had little in common, aside from being in the same class at school and living on the same street, and our childlike friendship required little to no work on my part, aside from the bike-pedaling or roller-skating it took to make my way over to her house. Few responsibilities limited our time together, few insecurities existed between us despite our differences, and little thought was given to where we stood with each other.

We just were.

High School and College Friendships

My family and I moved away from that street and that city entirely the summer between elementary school and middle school, that period of time that is the exact intersection of growing social awareness and self-conscious awkwardness. I cried my eyes out to my mom my entire sixth-grade year because I was the perpetual new kid, I didn't like being the new kid, and, most painfully of all, I was struggling to make new friends. It was the first time I'd ever felt out of place and, being brutally shy, I was suddenly faced with the realization that I'd actually have to *try* in order to have friends. Merely joining a softball team or the youth group at our new church wasn't going to cut it; I'd probably have to *speak* to people as well.

Finally, after about a year, I fell into a group of girls who were part of my youth group—Jo, Sara, Cindy, Ashley, and eventually Anne. It was Jo, however, who became my closest friend.

Jo knew when I liked a boy and I knew when she liked a boy, and, blessedly, we never liked the same ones. In middle and high school, not liking the same boys is absolutely the key to an enduring friendship, and so ours lasted. Together, we laid out in the summers, exercised to Jane Fonda aerobic videos, marched in the high school band, and slumber-partied at each other's houses, where we'd fall asleep listening to tapes of the New Kids On The Block.

Our friendship was comfortable, easy, and a warm, reassuring blanket during our high school years. Knowing I always had Jo, no matter what, gave me a sort of confidence that exceeded my average teenage insecurities.

Then came college. She chose one and I chose another, and we made plans as to how we'd stay connected. Our Sunday school teacher, with good intentions I'm sure, tried to prepare us for an evolving friendship, predicting that we probably wouldn't remain best friends. With that gauntlet thrown down, we entrenched ourselves even further in our dedication to call and write each week. Our mutual friend Nancy, who sat behind me in calculus class and constantly sprayed breath freshener into her mouth, informed me of something that might make communication easier—this thing called email.

"Oh no," I said snidely, "I'm sure that's not something I'll ever use."

Shockingly, we did use email. And the phone. And the answering machine. And old-fashioned letters. But mostly email, just as fresh-breathed Nancy said we would.

We weren't in close proximity anymore and our friendship required more work than it ever had, but I'd learned that friendship isn't always guaranteed, making friends takes effort, time together helps, being in each other's homes solidifies friendship, and I would have to let a friendship evolve in order for it to survive.

17

College is where I delved deeper into the distinctive joy and richness of Christian friendship. My freshman year I joined a Christian sorority made up of three hundred girls who "held me accountable" and asked me about "my walk" and wanted to "do life" with me. And did I mention that we had a counterpart Christian fraternity? I met my husband through that fraternity, and we were elected presidents of our respective groups at the same time. I'm not joking. We each had red presidential phones, hotlines that allowed us to call each other with Christian emergencies. OK, I'm joking about that one.

Christian community in college, I discovered, required a new kind of vulnerability. In high school, vulnerability was revealing the name of the boy you had a crush on. In college, however, there was the whole aforementioned accountability thing. People wanted to know stuff so they could pray for you. You listened to their stuff so you could pray for them. This was Christian friendship in college, cemented by intense time together, proximity, and lots and lots of fun. I found it incredibly fun to live with and among my friends and to stay up past midnight talking and laughing and even praying together. I enjoyed having a full social calendar and meeting hundreds of new and interesting people. (And, Mom and Dad, I also had a full academic calendar of studying, going to the library, getting eight hours of sleep each night, reading every assigned reading, and going to class. Yep, so, so full. PS: thanks for college. I learned a ton that I continue to use to this day.)

And Then We Became Adults

Looking back, college was the friendship jackpot. I remember that time with fondness, and I admit that I've spent much of my adulthood dreaming up ways to re-create that slice of life. College friendships felt much like my childhood friendships, when community just sort of happened to me, except in college it was with additional freedom, opportunities, and diversity in the types of friends I made. Everyone was on an equal playing field because everyone started as a new student and everyone was asking the same questions about life and the future and relationships.

But then we all became adults. Suddenly, we weren't on an equal playing field any longer, because some of us became engineers and some of us chose to get a graduate degree in psychology (ahem). Some of the kids I went to high school with had skipped college altogether, entering the workforce straight out of high school and having to grow up a little quicker. Some of us got married right away and some of us didn't. Some of us were already picking out fabric swatches for the curtains and couches in our newly purchased house while the rest of us went back to Mom and Dad's spare bedroom.

I moved into an apartment with Jo, who'd also graduated that May, and before we had even finished arranging the living room furniture she was blissfully and ecstatically engaged to the boy she'd giggled about through the computer back in college. Our boxes weren't even unpacked and she was already announcing that she'd be moving out in mere months. I was feeling less than blissful and ecstatic, because it felt like he was becoming her best friend and little single ol' me was being left in the dust.

I didn't like that my friendships were evolving, nor did I find this new social territory exciting. Life coaxed me toward making new friends, but I didn't want to make new friends; I simply wanted to figure out how to maintain the ones I already had. *I wanted things to be how they used to be.*

Effortless.

Carefree.

Fun.

In reality, I had crossed over some invisible line. I was no longer a child, and friendship had become inexplicably and frustratingly hard. The ease of childhood friendship was forever irretrievable.

———

Becoming an adult did a number on our friendships, did it not? At least that's what I've observed in my own life and what I've heard from other women along the way. Transitioning into life as an adult tilted our equilibrium in a way that took us *years* to recover from, if we've ever recovered at all. Finding and learning a new job, finding and learning a new city, finding and learning a new church, figuring out the whole singleness thing or the marriage-and-kids thing—all of these have demanded our best efforts and prime energy. Friendship? We've had to coast a little bit on what we built long ago, and, over time, all that coasting has ended in loneliness or attempts at re-creating youthful friendships or painful heartache and anguish. The ease and the confidence we'd grown up with regarding our ability to make and deepen friendships quietly eroded. The *time* we'd always enjoyed to make and deepen friendships evaporated into work and diapers.

Somehow, friendship became a struggle.

And I didn't have the foggiest clue how to cultivate adult friendships. They seemed a different creature altogether, and they definitely would require work and effort—I could tell that the second I crossed the invisible line into adulthood—but just how was I going to do this? How did one make new friends and spend time with old ones while also juggling so many responsibilities and obligations?

Inching along in traffic every day as I commuted to my first post-college job, I thought about the adult friendships I'd observed growing up, searching for clues. Honestly, there weren't many friendships I could recall, and that should have been my first clue.

But there was one.

When I was a child, my parents constantly lugged my sister and me across town to Kay and Kenny's house. There, we played with their son, ate simple meals, and ran wildly through the mishmash of yards in their home's vicinity while our parents talked or played cards. I don't remember *not* knowing Kay and Kenny. They'd been my parents' friends since before my birth.

When my family moved across Texas that summer before I started middle school, Kay and Kenny actually moved with us. When Kay and Kenny built a house on a cul-de-sac, we built a house right across the street. When their son got his driver's license, he became my ride to and from school each day. Even when the three of us kids were teenagers and all going our separate directions, we still occasionally had hamburgers on Kay and Kenny's back porch and we still went to the lake together each summer.

Even then—the summer after college, which I spent sitting in Dallas traffic—when I'd go home to visit, soon after I pulled into the driveway, Kay and Kenny would come across the street with a meal or an invitation for dessert on their back porch, as if their own child had come home.

Their friendship with my parents had taken purposefulness: they'd made decisions that stoked the friendship and kept it alive. These decisions weren't necessarily as big as the one to move to the same city at the same time, although that certainly helped, but rather smaller ones: to pop into each other's homes for a few minutes of conversation, to serve at church together, to champion each other's children.

Their friendship had also taken perseverance: they didn't quit on each other, despite being fairly different and despite their children being fairly different. And it had taken time. Their friendship had been built over many years, not a few months. Like with a good wine, time had aged the friendship well.

As a fledgling grown-up, searching for clues about adult friendship, I knew instinctively that this kind of friendship was rare, and, thinking about it for the first time, I treasured that my parents had cultivated such a thing and that, simply by proximity and osmosis, I'd had it too. I'd had the picnics on the back deck thrown together at the last minute and the spontaneous decisions to go out to eat, all of us piling intermixed into cars. We just walked into their house and they just walked into ours, bringing or borrowing whatever was needed. And if we were lucky, the meal ended with Kenny's famous homemade ice cream, the kind that is half-melted from the start and requires a second or third helping.

On the back door of the house where Kay and Kenny lived when I was young hung a sign that read, "Back-door friends are best."

That's what I hoped for myself: back-door friends, women who felt comfortable waltzing in my door without knocking, who grabbed what they needed from my fridge without asking permission, who knew that there was a seat at the table and love in my heart for them, and who knew that the meal just might end with homemade ice cream.

And so, with those clues and hopes and ideals in my head, I set out to get that kind of adult friendship.

TWO

The Dreams We Have for Friendship

Christian brotherhood is not an ideal which we must realize; it is rather a reality created by God in Christ in which we may participate.

Dietrich Bonhoeffer[1]

*Y*esterday I heard a classic Journey song on the radio, the one about bright lights, life on the road, and intense pining for a love waiting at home. ("I'm forever yours, faithfully."[2])

In high school, when Jo and I traveled with the marching band to away football games, I listened to that song over and over again on my Walkman, dreaming of the time when I'd finally have a love to call my own. I suppose I thought at the time that I was living a hard life on the road, traveling to play my flute because our football team needed rallying, and that, somewhere, someone was faithfully waiting for me to high-step into the stadium of his heart.

When I heard the song yesterday, I was driving my mom car to pick up my kids at school for the bazillionth day in a row. I'd spent the morning doing laundry and dishes, making copies for a meeting I was leading at church on Sunday, responding to emails, cleaning toilets to prepare for hosting small group, and briefly talking to my husband on the phone in order to discuss car repairs. In other words, an enviously sexy morning. So sexy I'd forgotten to eat breakfast, and food is not something I ever forget to do. Rather than a romantic music video, I instead seemed to be auditioning for a *Saturday Night Live* sketch about mom jeans.

Those first few keyboard notes of "Faithfully" hit my speakers, however, and I was transported back—not to high school, not to the constricting feeling of those polyester band pants and my pretend music videos, but to a deep sense of *longing*. I longed again for what I'd dreamed of in high school: an all-encompassing, undistracted love. I longed in that moment to escape my life and my responsibilities, even for a few short hours, and be enveloped by a romantic escapade with my husband. Not only that—and I knew this was asking a lot—but I really wanted that time with my husband to be free of car repair decisions. I wanted the rapturous, the romantic, the music video (minus the mullets) kind of love.

Instead, I sat in the carpool line and then oh-so-rapturously made spaghetti for dinner.

I have been married for seventeen years. I know from experience that the romantic ideal of love is a cloud of smoke that dissipates quickly. However, I know what long-standing, everyday love is, and I know that it's so much better than anything Journey ever made me believe.

But sometimes, especially when I'm knee-deep in the routines and obligations of life, the fantasy beckons loudly and seems to be of greater glory than reality, and I have to remind myself that to hold on to a dream is to miss the beauty of real love.

In other words, I tend toward thinking that the ideal is still the dream even though I know it's not the dream.

God began shattering my romanticized, me-centered dream of marriage on our honeymoon, but there was another romanticized dream I held tightly to my chest for much longer into my adult life: friendship. The dream I'd set out to get, born in rush-hour traffic on I-75 during a summer of discontent and grief over all that had changed, backstopped by easy childhood and college friendships. It became a longing; I longed for ideal friendship and earnestly believed it was possible. It was a longing for what I imagined friendship could be, what I hoped it would be, and I clutched it for years, unwilling to release it, convinced everyone had it but me.

The Search for the One True Friend to Rule Them All

Let's fast-forward from my first year out of college, when I was figuring out life in the real world. I got married a few years later, and a year into our marriage my husband, Kyle, accepted a church staff position in the town where we'd attended college, so we moved, bought a house, and, a few years after that, had the first of our three children. My college friends were scattered, Jo and her husband had moved across the country, and I was left trying to form adult friendships in the town I'd known only as a college student.

I didn't try very hard, if you want to know the truth.

We lived in that town for seven years, and those were some of the loneliest years of my life. I'm not sure I had a single friend, at least not one I felt comfortable calling to take care of my kids if I came down with anything more serious than a cold. That was my litmus test—*Who would I call in an emergency? Who would I call if I needed something?* The answer was a shrug, which always elicited a pang in my heart.

Friendship—or the lack thereof—became a source of insecurity, pain, and even shame, because it was so starkly different from what it had been in other periods in my life. Somewhere along the way, I figured, I'd lost the ability to make friends. I felt as if I was moving backward, as if I was forgetting important things I'd felt so sure about for most of my life.

Before you begin feeling sorry for me or, probably more so, wanting to punch me in my whiny, self-pitying face, I readily admit that my loneliness was *all my fault*. I can see it all so clearly now, although at the time I couldn't see any of it. I couldn't see that I was too much inside myself and frustrated that people didn't pursue me. I couldn't see that my response to the frustration—isolating myself physically and emotionally and rarely pursuing anyone—was hurting me further. I didn't notice how, when people would ask me to do this or that, I'd say no because it didn't fit into my nice, neat little box of time and interest and ease.

One woman, I remember, would ask me to join her and her friend for lunch while my son was at Mother's Day Out, and I rejected the invitation over and over because I had errands to run. *Errands, for crying out loud.* I didn't take into account how very rarely I asked anyone to lunch or coffee or over to our house. I didn't see how, when I actually did reach out to people, I kept things very much on the surface because I was afraid to be vulnerable with people.

Throughout those years there were sputtering starts and, when things didn't immediately blossom into deep friendship, abrupt stops. I didn't ask for help, I didn't lean on anyone, and I didn't let anyone see me sweat. I don't know why I behaved that way; it went against everything I'd learned in my formative friendships about time and hospitality and vulnerability.

Friendship became something that elicited shame, but, at the same time, I craved it with Journey-like intensity. I couldn't find words for it but I often found myself in tears. Only my husband saw my tears, and most of them in those years were related to friendship.

Really, I was insecure and nervous and arrogant, because now that I can look back at those years with matured vision, I recognize that I actually had seedling friendships during the very times I was in tears over my want. I couldn't name my friends then because I couldn't see them, but I can name them now: Ashley and Jamee and Niki and Kelly. Ashley and I had a raw conversation about our children at the pool one day that swung wide the door for friendship. Jamee and I had a standing playdate. Niki offered me encouragement when I needed it, and Kelly was always so easy to be with. But I wasn't satisfied, to be honest. I wanted something more while at the same time doing nothing to *have* more.

I can also now understand why I couldn't see those friendships for the gifts they were—because my vision was blurred by my romanticized, idealistic standard of that One True Friend to Rule Them All.

My own dream, though it seemed beautiful and attainable, was actually piercing me through. My dream by its very nature held prerequisite stipulations: my one true friend needed to live in my town, attend my church, be married and have children, have a husband whom my husband liked, and be a friend who empathetically understood the demands ministry placed upon us. My friendships were the equivalent of Jerry's dating rotation on *Seinfeld*: I rejected perfectly good seedling relationships because of ridiculous and petty details such as Man Hands. Or, in my case, age, marital status, or a so-so conversation.

Can I tell you, as I look back at that time, what I so clearly see now? In my desire to have good friends, I'd simply traded one immature perspective of friendship from my childhood—that friendship would simply happen to me—for another: that the perfect friendship was actually attainable.

The Wish-Dream

Perfect (and easy) friendship seems to be the last-to-die dream for many women. We see through the smoke of romantic love fairly early, we learn quickly that chasing beauty or money or perfection is like grasping for the wind, but we hold oh so tightly to our ideal dream of friendship.

Dietrich Bonhoeffer calls this our wish-dream. In his book *Life Together*, he says we all have wish-dreams about life in Christian community: "The serious Christian, set down for the first time in a Christian community, is likely to bring with him a very definite idea of what Christian life together should be and to try to realize it."[3] We must be aware of the desires we attach to Christian friendship, he says, because "in Christian brotherhood everything depends upon its being clear right from the beginning, first, that Christian brotherhood is not an ideal, but a divine reality."[4]

Unfortunately, we Christians seem to be the most stubborn purveyors of the wish-dream, because it sounds biblical to pursue idealistic unity and community. Friendship doesn't happen according to our dream world, however. It's not linear or static or formulaic. Friendship is formed between imperfect people among the concrete and messy realities of life. Biblical friendship is distinct in that it brings the grace, forgiveness, and truth of Jesus into those messy realities, but it is messy nevertheless. Just as marital love is forged in the daily acts of care and selflessness and mundane responsibilities, friendship is formed in real life—sin, suffering, conflict, and all.

Bonhoeffer seems to be saying to us that friendship is a good and right desire, but it is only able to be given and received as God intended it to be given and received—and he deals in reality rather than a dream world. We aren't asked to give up our desire for friendship, only the *immature* version of it—that all will be hippy-skippy perfect, that relationships will be forever fun and easy, that we can sit back and wait for others to come toward us, and that all of our needs will be met through other people.

We need only become aware of the wish-dream and we'll suddenly see it writing itself all over our hearts. That's why I can look back and see those years so clearly. Because now I know about the wish-dream.

I recently gathered together some of my friends—friends from all different ages and stages—and asked them about their own perspectives on friendship. Their wish-dreams immediately came to the surface.

Lacy: An aspect of friendship that I have longed for and struggled to find or know if I already have it—maybe I have it but I don't realize it—is that friend who just knows . . . or that friend who, if something really crazy happened with my kids or at home, would be that first friend I call. I've thought about that before. A lot of times I haven't known who that is. Maybe I do have that friend, but maybe I've idealized who that person should be, so I don't recognize who those people are in my life.

Susan: I think we sometimes still think like children: it should be easy, it should be one person, and this person is going to be everything to me. And it hasn't turned out to be that way. Friendships take a ton of work.

Marylyn: For me, it's not just wondering who I'm going to call but wondering who's going to call me. And I want that to be the same person. So often the person who calls me isn't the person I'm going to call.

Kate: There was a stage when we lived with another married couple. I remember thinking it would be awesome. *We'll cook dinner together* *and go grocery shopping together! It's going to be like we're in college with roommates but we're married! This is going to be wonderful! Let's live in community together!* Week two, I thought, *I don't know if God really called me to this community.* We had to push through raw pain and conflict. I wanted to quit almost every month. As women, we want to quit when it gets hard. We think, *This isn't easy, so maybe I misinterpreted it.* For that period in my life, it was obvious that God called me to that friendship. He made it apparent and clear. That didn't make it easy.

Amy D: Part of my wish-dream is that I wish I could *be* the perfect friend.

Melanie: Too often I think, *Oh, I want her to be my friend because we would have so much in common.* Even if "her" is someone who isn't really available to friendship, so to speak. It is also true that sometimes I don't think of people as friends who really are because they are a co-worker or older or younger. I definitely have an ideal friendship in my mind—the relationship I had with my best friend in high school. That is sort of the relationship I apply the word *friend* to, but it isn't a practical type of relationship for most women. So maybe I need to be more generous with the label *friend*.

Emma: I think we all desire a comfy, closed circle with our BFFs, with no one who's hard to love or who doesn't fit in. I think we often have unrealistic expectations for friendships.

Wish-Dreams Hinder Real Friendship

I see myself in their words. I see how I've pierced myself through with my own wish-dream, all because I've dealt in idealism rather than reality.

Do you see the wish-dream in your own heart? Take note of its shape and be quick to release it, because the wish-dream is not inconsequential. It is a hindrance to *real* friendship. When we hold an ideal of friendship in our minds, believing it's attainable, we hold a standard above the heads of real women God has placed in our lives, and then we wonder why we're constantly disappointed by the realities, complexities, and difficulties in our relationships.

That was me. In the season of life when I had few friends, my wish-dream fed my disappointment with myself and with others, but primarily with God. It appeared to me that everyone around me had friends; therefore, I concluded God was withholding a good gift from me for no apparent reason. Even now that I am all too aware of my tendency toward idealizing friendship and what I think it should be, my wish-dreams resurrect themselves: I want to keep friendships static; I don't want people to move or change or make decisions that hinder us from getting together. I am a mother hen, trying desperately to gather my friends in a little cozy cage and keep them there forever. Lovingly, of course.

I want the sugary-sweet, easy-come community where we flit into one another's homes without knocking, laugh deep into the night, know one another and are known without effort, and never exchange a cross or challenging word. I typically envision dinner parties and game nights, vacationing together and talking on the phone every day.

It seems this is a common idea of what Christian community should be. It seems that to let it go is to let go of a right and good dream, a biblical dream of unity and community. But in reality, our wish-dreams have little to do with God and his kingdom and everything to do with us and ours. God gives us relationships that are enjoyable and a blessing but also sanctify and challenge us out of our selfishness, because he intends to get the glory from our friendships. Our wish-dreams encourage us to seek our own glory and satisfaction in friendships that are safe, easy, comfortable, and self-serving.

I want the dinner parties and the game nights and the vacations and every cozy scenario I can think of because I want to feel a sense of security and belonging in this world, and I don't necessarily want to have to sacrifice, serve, and love without being served and loved in return. I want the Instagram picture of friendship, not the three-dimensional, real-life kind.

Although my wish-dream appears beautiful, I tell myself it's like a puff of cotton candy that disappears on my tongue. As long as I feed the dream, I will be left with just a film of disappointment and dissatisfaction.

Our wish-dreams must die a painful death so that we can get on with real-life friendship.

Wish-dreams don't want to be reminded of real life, where friendship takes effort and there is precious little time and responsibilities often come first and physical distance exists. Wish-dreams don't envision the faithful wounds of a friend or walking with them through death or mental illness. No, wish-dreams reach forward or reach back for anything that's not reality, prettying it all up, romanticizing it like a Journey song, and making it all seem maddeningly attainable.

Consequences of Wish-Dreams

If we do not shatter our wish-dreams of friendship, God, in his grace, always will. He desires to give us true, biblical friendship, and it all hangs on how we respond when our romanticized view of friendship is trampled on. Will we look inward with a critical eye, blaming ourselves? Will we look outward with judgment and frustration, blaming those around us for their insensitivity and callousness? Will we give God the stink-eye until he gives the good gift he appears to be withholding from us? Will we hold tightly to the shattered pieces of our dreams and either try to piece them back together or bemoan in isolation what we clutch in our hands? Will we allow our shattered wish-dreams to feed our insecurities, comparison, and bitterness and keep us from using our gifts to serve others?

Bonhoeffer says these are the natural consequences of the wish-dream: "The man who fashions a visionary ideal of community demands that it be realized by God, by others, and by himself. He enters the community of Christians with his demands, sets up his own law, and judges the brethren and God Himself accordingly. . . . When things do not go his way, he calls the effort a failure. . . . So he becomes, first an accuser of his brethren, then an accuser of God, and finally the despairing accuser of himself."[5]

When I first read those words, they pierced me to the heart. They encapsulated the years stretching from college to when I had three small children underfoot. They helped me to finally see why friendship had been so difficult—because I had made it about me and my own personalized vision of what I wanted it to look like. Over and over and over again, I'd tried to piece together a wish-dream God had shattered.

And so I learned a vital lesson that has served me far more than any others I'd picked up in my formative years: true friendship is mapped out by God and it is for him. A rich opportunity for friendship exists when we reject the ideal wish-dream, understand God's design for friendship, and embrace those imperfect women who are right in front of us.

This perspective wiped my slate clean, freeing me from my childish and selfish perspective, but it was put to the test soon after.

After seven years in that city where I had so struggled, we moved to a different state because of a new ministry calling and I made a conscious choice that I wouldn't pack my wish-dream along with the baby crib and the china. God was giving me a friendship do-over, and I determined to learn from my false starts, mistakes, and all those seedling friendships I'd never truly watered.

Eight years after that move, I am still no expert. In fact, I've made a mess of some of my relationships and I'm still not always sure about myself when it comes to friendship. But I no longer romanticize it. My apologies to Journey, but I *have* stopped believin'—in the cotton-candy dream. I can say, as someone who has left the shattered wish-dream shattered, that there *is* a way to cultivate beautiful real-life friendships, messiness and all.

Remember what Bonhoeffer said? Christian brotherhood is not an ideal, but it is a *divine reality*.

It starts there.

THREE

How God Gives Friendship

A man who has friends must himself be friendly, but there is a
friend who sticks closer than a brother.

Proverbs 18:24

This past summer my friend Amy and I made our annual day trip
to the beach. We'd made the drive several times, both separately
and together, so, without a lick of planning or forethought, figuring we
knew the route, we stuffed my children and all of our beach gear in the
car and set off. With the kids pacified in the backseat, Amy and I started
talking and didn't stop until two hours later when, I supposed, we were
almost there and should start figuring out where we could park. Amy
plugged our destination into her phone and said incredulously, "It says
we still have an hour left to go."

"That's weird," I said. "I feel like we should be getting there right
about now. It didn't take us this long last year, did it?"

And then, placing our blind trust in the occasional instruction of the
GPS voice, we returned to talking.

Thirty minutes later, doubt percolating in my mind, I once again
considered our destination and said to Amy, "Let me see where we are
according to your phone."

She held out her phone so I could pinpoint the little blue dot on the map, pulsing happily but in an unexpected spot. I looked more closely, puzzled, until I realized that we had literally been driving in circles, making a loop around the exit we needed to take in order to get to the beach. Sure enough, within the next few miles we approached signs for a tunnel we'd already driven through an hour earlier. The kids, right on cue, piped up from the backseat: "Are we there yet? When are we going to get to the beach? Wait, weren't we just here?"

We should have already been at the beach by that point, lazing in the sun, but instead we were passing familiar billboards for law offices and seafood restaurants and kicking ourselves for navigating by instinct rather than carefully plotting our route on the map. Because we hadn't done so, we'd added more than an hour and lots of unnecessary frustration to our drive.

I can't count the number of times I've heard an eerily similar frustration from women about friendship. They feel like they're driving in circles, trying to reach a destination they're not sure how to reach, spent by discouragement and frustration and hurts. The problem stems from their reliance on instinct rather than a carefully charted course based upon Scripture.

Instinct tells us our friendship struggles are all our fault. *Shame.*

Instinct tells us the fault lies with the church or the circle of women we observe with envy. *Bitterness.*

Instinct tells us to sit back and wait for someone to come toward us. *Passivity and isolation.*

Can I tell you something? Every single woman struggles with friendship. Every. Single. One. I know this because, as a pastor's wife, I have a vantage point that allows me to see and hear the big picture. Two of the greatest commonalities I hear from women who confide in me is that they fear everyone is hanging out without them and they've felt deeply wounded by other women. They are surprised and disbelieving when I tell them all women struggle with these things. Instinct has lied to them and told them they're the only ones.

Facebook and Instagram generate the absolute worst taunts when our minds are tangled up in the belief that we're the only ones. When I see a picture of two people I know hanging out, my reflexive thought is, *Why wasn't I invited?* Even if I barely know those people. Even if they are hanging out clear across the country. Even if in reality I'm not all that interested in actually hanging out. *I just want to be chosen and loved.* We all do.

So we can't rely on instinct, blindly seeking our destination of friendship based on feel. We mustn't look for God to frame friendship in the way we design; we must look to him and discover the map he's already given. Otherwise we will chase dreams and feelings-driven experiences and shun the realities that true, God-given community requires.

It's necessary to return to the map, I've discovered, because our instincts only build our wish-dreams and keep us circling the right exit but never finding our destination. Also, an instinctual approach to friendship is a fleshly, worldly approach, leading to frustration, anger, bitterness, isolation, persistent ideal-seeking, and—many times—giving up on people entirely. Rather than approaching friendship according to our instinctual wish-dreams, we must look at what Bonhoeffer calls the divine reality—the map God has provided to show us what friendship is, how to discover it, and how to navigate toward deepening relationships.

What we'll find is that our exit is closer than we often think; we just have to be willing to take it.

The Starting and Ending Point

First, we notice our navigation on the map is circular: biblical friendship begins with God and ends with him also.

Friendship began with God extending his hand toward humanity. In the very beginning, he sought out the company of the people he'd created, walking with them in the garden.

Even after sin entered the world and the dream world we still seek was leveled, he selected people to be his friends: Abraham and Moses. These patriarchs were allowed unique and awe-inspiring privileges of friendship—God spoke to Moses in private conversation and gave Abraham the title of his friend forever.[1] Their friendship with God, however, wasn't selective and insular. This intimacy with God gave birth to great responsibility, for God intended his friendship with these men (through their callings, gifts, and righteousness) to extend the blessing to others. With Abraham, for instance, he said, "I will bless you and make your name great; and you shall be a blessing" (Gen. 12:2). This serves as an important navigational tool on our map about the nature and goal of our friendships—and all relationships for that matter—but let's not get ahead of ourselves.

Like ripples extending outward on a pond, God grew his circle of friendship ever wider. Through Jesus's life, death, and resurrection, he extended the offer of friendship to all people, offering reconciliation between God and humanity to anyone who would come to him by faith. *Friendship* is almost too trivial a word for what Christ offers, for we are certainly not his peers. However, the word *friend* does convey the delight of the Father in those he's befriended, the companionship available to us in Christ, the moment-to-moment help we have in the Holy Spirit, and the enjoyment we can find in God even in the mundane routines of life. Through Jesus, there is nothing left between God and us that hinders our intimacy as friends—no wrath, no disappointment, no ritual, no condemnation. If ever we sought a wish-dream, this is it—and, thankfully, profound intimacy with the greatest Friend is no longer a dream but a sure reality.

And so friendship begins here, where God has extended himself toward us. We receive his friendship by submitting to him and also by positioning ourselves as enemies of the world and its ways.[2] Through Christ, we have access to all we need for life and godliness, or as the classic hymn understates, "What a friend we have in Jesus!"[3] This is John's teaching in 1 John when he describes the Christ he's seen and experienced. He invites us into the fellowship of Christ, saying, "Truly our fellowship is with the Father and with His Son Jesus Christ."[4] Afterward, a by-product appears: "If we walk in the light as He is in the light, we have fellowship with one another."[5] Fellowship with God leads to friendship with others. Friendship, then, is a gift from our Father, and we're right to give it and receive it with joy.

He didn't just win us friendship; Christ also teaches us how to be a friend. Jesus's life on earth gives us a framework, a map, for engaging others. We see how he's related to us so we, like Abraham and Moses, can take what he's given us and extend the blessing to others.

Intersections

The second aspect we notice about our map are intersections. As we receive God's friendship, he intersects us with others so that we might, like Abraham, be a blessing. He says to us, "This is my friend also," and joins us together as we journey. Or he points to one he is calling to be his friend and asks us to walk alongside them, displaying the friendship Christ is offering them.

This is called the fellowship of Christ, where our common rallying point is his gospel.[6]

There are no parameters as to whom God intersects our lives with, although we are prone to erect them according to our instinctual and worldly wish-dreams. If we accept God's design, he allows us the privilege and joy of intersecting with others from different races, nationalities, life stages, ages, backgrounds, and marital statuses.

However, there are parameters given as to what *manner* we intersect with them. They are fellow sojourners, nothing more, nothing less. In fact, there are warning signs and even flashing lights along the way, reminding us not to become confused. God is God and people are people.

In the rest of this book, we'll dig deeper into just *how* we give and receive friendship, but it's important to note that as much as we are called into fellowship with others, we must never move our gaze of hope and longing away from fellowship with God. He is guaranteed—a sure and steady anchor for our souls—and he is the perfect Friend.

In our wish-dreams, we tend to make people our gods. We look to them—at least I have—to know us intimately at all times, to meet our every need, to be there when we want them near, and to love us unconditionally and perfectly, when the map points only to God as having these abilities.

When I am disappointed with my friendships and I take time to dig a little deeper in my heart, I inevitably find that I'm looking for my friends to relate to me as only God can. I want God to give me good friends, and when he has, I've been prone to shove him aside for the attention, wisdom, and companionship of those friends, despite knowing that they were intended as gifts rather than replacements. People are not fillers for a present God, and God is not a placeholder for future friends.

Thankfully and incredibly, God loves differently than human beings love one another. He is not hindered or limited in his understanding or love. He loves us intimately. All those feelings bombarding us concerning our life situation? All those thoughts we wrestle with? All those struggles to comprehend and difficulties to navigate? He knows them even more thoroughly than we can articulate them to ourselves, much less to others.

St. Augustine describes God as being "closer to me than I am to myself."[7] Because he knows us intimately he also comforts us intimately. He fully enters our pain because, unlike most friends, he can fully handle its weight, emotion, and complexity. We can go to him and be understood. And that is where our pain is eased. From him, we gather strength to face another day. Through him, we see others with his eyes and we realize that everyone has pain, and, like him, we reach out to others. In him, peace finds a dwelling place in our souls.

I don't know what you face today, but it is probably something specific to you and your life. Whether in circumstances big or small, I hope you enjoy the comfort of godly, loving friends and family. But when they aren't enough—because they never will be—I hope you will run to the Friend who loves you with a perfect love.

Our Destination

Although God is our only perfect Friend, we're invited into a life filled with people, so it's helpful to ask ourselves: What is the goal of friendship?

Where is this map directing us? How will we know when we've arrived at the proper destination of biblical friendship?

God has invited us into the fellowship of Christ, which is what we call the church. He has given us to one another in the larger church, yet within the larger we will most often interact with the smaller. Like Jesus with James, Peter, and John, this is the category of friendship—those within the closest concentric circle, those with access and proximity to us and us to them.

Our destination or goal is not to arrive at a static, linear version of friendship where we get all of our relationships lined up just so and keep them that way for a lifetime. No, the goal of friendship is to secure ourselves to the sure, steadfast anchor of Christ and, while holding to that anchor, give and receive the gift of friendship as we have opportunity. The goal is to enjoy God together with others and, as we move through life, to sharpen and allow ourselves to be sharpened by friends. We imitate Jesus with one another, willing to face the stark realities and consequences of sin, all the while persevering in our efforts to offer love, grace, forgiveness, reconciliation, comfort, and care to one another. In doing so, we display to one another and the world how God loves and, through this, bring him glory. This is our destination, the point on the map we move toward: bringing God glory.

Bonhoeffer says:

> It is easily forgotten that the fellowship of Christian brethren is a gift of grace, a gift of the Kingdom of God that any day may be taken from us, that the time that still separates us from utter loneliness may be brief indeed. Therefore, let him who until now has had the privilege of living a common Christian life with other Christians praise God's grace from the bottom of his heart. Let him thank God on his knees and declare: It is grace, nothing but grace, that we are allowed to live in community with Christian brethren.[8]

A gift of grace, both to give and to receive. This is God's dream for us.

Therefore, we must not give up on dreams of friendship, because it's evident that friendship is a good and godly desire, even an imperative, yet we must be careful that our dreams align with God's. The sense of struggle we feel in relationships, the sense of physical and emotional separation we experience—we must recognize these feelings as a longing for the perfection and beauty of heaven. It's a longing for Christ and the final redemption he offers, and it's a longing to live and move and breathe as he does toward us. This is a beautiful desire, not something we should feel ashamed to have. But we must bring this desire to God and learn to trust and receive from him. We must, like with any good gift, hold this desire in its proper place and appreciate what he has given us right now, even if what he's given is not necessarily what we envision.

A good, biblical friendship actually brings us to that place of longing, because the map navigates us back around to God. It begins with God because all truth begins with him and because friendship was his idea in the first place; it ends with God because biblical friendship points us back to him and stirs our anticipation of unmarred, heavenly relationships with our Father and with others.

In the present, the road on our map is bumpy and broken. Enjoying the gift of friendship in the midst of bumpy and broken is what makes it distinctly Christian, however, and also distinctly and dazzlingly beautiful.

FOUR

Messy Beautiful Friendship

When the morning mists of dreams vanish, then dawns the bright day of Christian fellowship.

Dietrich Bonhoeffer[1]

The words came through an email, and, as I'd skimmed through, I at first assumed I hadn't read them correctly. My heart began beating quickly as I reread the first few lines and saw that, in fact, I'd read them right the first time. The biting words sunk in deep. A friend had misunderstood me and not given me the benefit of the doubt, and she was writing to let me know I had disappointed her.

We've all been hurt by someone we considered a friend, whether it's an inconsiderate word or an unexpected betrayal. I've discovered that when it happens to me, as it did through that email, it's my natural tendency, like that of many others, to pull away, erect protective barriers around my vulnerability, and let the friendship fade into the background as if it never existed.

Sometimes, when the wound is especially deep, our tendency is not just to write the friend off but also to write *friendship* off. We're hurt so badly that we give ourselves over to cynicism, bitterness, and resentment and we wonder if friendship is worth the risk of wading through the emotions and hurts, attempting reconciliation, and making ourselves vulnerable again. We are friendly and sociable at a safe distance, but heart-level friendship? It's too hard and too risky, or, as we've already established, it never quite lives up to our exacting wish-dreams. With that ideal view in mind, it's far too easy to feel insecure about or frustrated with reality.

I tend to want to cast the responsibility or the blame for my imperfect friendships on others, but it works both ways. Sometimes I am the one who hurts others, something I inadvertently did this year. Although my friend whom I hurt brought it to my attention, at first I remained blind to the way I was wounding her, wanting to blame her instead. But she brought it to my attention again, just as clear and gentle as the first time, and I finally saw what my protective barriers had kept me from seeing and how they had been used as weapons instead of defense. This friend challenged me to stay in the friendship and work through our differences rather than keep my distance, something that felt risky to me but in the end has been worth it and, I know, honors the Lord.

Isn't this what true, biblical friendship is about: being willing to love, forgive, and bear with those we might not necessarily always understand? And being willing to confess sin, inadvertent or not, and receive the grace that helps us grow? This is certainly more what it's about than dinner parties and game nights. Biblical friendship is what helps us grow; it sharpens us just as we are used by God to sharpen others.[2]

Over coffee, a young woman in my church and I discussed these things together, about how we have this stubborn belief that friendship can actually be what we ideally picture in our heads. She said she wished people would invite her to more things and talked about how it seemed like everyone was always getting together without her. I said I sometimes envied certain relationships and resented that I wasn't included in them. After confessing our self-focused thoughts to each other, our conversation turned to what true friendship is and what it looks like in reality.

Isn't it, we said, an ongoing effort? Doesn't it require commitment and perseverance? Isn't it having to deal biblically with our inevitable hurts, being quick to forgive, crossing life-stage boundaries, and refusing to put other women in categories? Isn't it pushing through discomfort and refusing to give up on people even when they disappoint us? And perhaps the most important question: Isn't it the greater blessing to *be* a person who seeks this type of community rather than clinging to false ideals and waiting for it to just "happen" to us?

While it *is* a greater blessing, we determined that it's also risky. We must look to serve rather than be served, which means it's possible that we might not be served in the ways we hope. We must be ever willing to broaden the circle, which means we must have an eye for the outsider rather than an eye for how we can be insiders, and it's possible we might be forgotten in the process. We must be willing to address sin and conflict in an appropriate way, which means it's possible we might be rejected. We must be willing to be vulnerable, which means we might be misunderstood and grace might not be extended to us.

Instead of holding fast to our ideals, we need to cling to a new definition of friendship, one that allows for awkwardness and risk and fumbling through, because isn't the road of true friendship paved by these very things? Paul offers us a definition for friendship that we'd do better to cling to than our false ideals:

> Therefore, as the elect of God, holy and beloved, put on tender mercies, kindness, humility, meekness, longsuffering; bearing with one another, and forgiving one another, if anyone has a complaint against another; even as Christ forgave you, so you also must do. But above all these things, put on love, which is the bond of perfection. And let the peace of God rule in your hearts, to which also you were called in one body; and be thankful. (Col. 3:12–15)

Paul certainly goes beyond vacationing together and making small talk and waiting for someone else to initiate. He exhorts us to *actively pursue* being a godly friend to others—to *actively pursue* being patient, forgiving, loving, and being thankful for others as we relate to them. The focus is on what we give to others, not what they give to us. We don't do these things because we hope to get something in return, friendship or whatever else. We do these things because that is how Christ showed his love toward us and because biblical friendship will always model itself after him.

Until heaven, our community will never be perfect; it's inevitable that we will experience hurt and disappointment in our relationships. *But it's worth the risk.* By actively pursuing others the way Christ pursues us, we extend an invitation for the friendship we desire but we also discover the beautiful and always-faithful way in which Christ relates to us. Because we have an anchor that's sure and steadfast, because we recognize friendship as a gift, we're willing to embrace the reality of friendship—messiness and all.

This is what Bonhoeffer meant when he said Christian community is not a dream but a divine reality: when we engage in relationships with our eyes wide open both to Christ as our Friend and to the realities of how sin and human weakness mar friendship, we're able to experience fuller and healthier friendships. We're bound together by our common Friend and our commitment to him, not by the gifts he gives or the experiences we hope for.

The Realities of Friendship

If we're committed to navigating friendship biblically instead of living in a dream world, we will at some point face stark realities.

The very first and often most difficult reality to accept is this: friendship is not easy. In fact, it can be a profound struggle. When we come up against this struggle, will we persevere or will we give up?

My friend Jenny recently confessed her private struggle with friendship, even her frustration toward me. As we walked together, it took her awhile to get the words out. "I'm so embarrassed, so ashamed at my thoughts," she said, hesitating after she'd asked if she could be honest with me. Finally, she expressed that she was finding friendship difficult, that she had been plagued by insecurities and unwanted bitterness. She felt ashamed that friendship wasn't easy for her.

Living on this planet means that relationships will be marred by sin, which means no one has it easy. As I told Jenny, we don't have to be ashamed that we find friendship difficult at times. We mustn't be afraid to look those difficulties in the face; our difficulty actually has something to say to us about our need for God's help in it, and if we look away, we're prone to give up and miss God's sanctifying work in our lives.

And that's it exactly: when we give up on friendship or specific friendships, we actually resist the gift of God's sanctification in our lives and being that gift in the lives of other women. The difficulty is actually part of the design, but we avoid it at all costs and, in avoiding it, we miss out on the beauty of Christian friendship. When we persevere through difficulty in friendship, however, we discover something valuable: God has changed and grown us through our friends and we've been the iron that has sharpened them in turn.

Don't be afraid to look this reality in the face either: friends will disappoint us. Those whom we love the most and who love us the most will disappoint us at some point, if they haven't already. They will even hurt us deeply at times. And guess what? We're going to hurt our friends too. Our friends will fail us, and we'll fail them. This reality of biblical friendship has something to say to us as well, if we're willing to look at it full in the face: God didn't design friendship to be our all-in-all. In fact, any time we try to hold up friendship as a guarantee or a necessity, God will tear down that idol.

Just yesterday, I hosted a going-away party for my friend Kate, who is relocating to a different state with her family. We had a time of blessing and commissioning for them, but I honestly was in a fog of denial throughout the party. I know it's happening—they're moving in a little over a week—but if I don't think about it, maybe everything will magically stay the same. Maybe it won't hurt.

I asked Kate about her own feelings. She said she feels a lot of fear about moving, because her friendships will be severed in a way that's not her choice. It's a hurt she can't control. The losses feel really deep, because she knows how hard it is to maintain friendships with people right in front of her, and it's even harder when they're thousands of miles away.

I don't want her to go, because I know that our relationship will change. I won't be able to meet her for coffee or have her and her family over for dinner. I won't get to watch her kids grow up, the kind of watching that's mostly unaware because you see them every week. Instead, I'll watch them grow in giant spurts and marvel at the passage of time each time they visit.

I know, though, that what I'm afraid of is the actual longing, because I know too well what it's like to live with longing.

We *all* know that feeling, because part of friendship is living with longing, and I don't mean just longing for a friend when you aren't sure you have any. A right and biblical perspective on life leaves us in an in-between place where all is made right and fulfilled because of Christ and all is waiting for that ultimate fulfillment to become tangible and visible. Friendship is included in that in-between because, although we are reconciled and united by Christ, we continue to relate to one another through the fog of flesh, sin, separation, and death.

Embrace Friendship as God Gives It

The stark realities of friendship are not something to mourn, only something to acknowledge, because as I've already hinted at, all of these realities have something beautiful and good to whisper to us. Things about God as our Friend. Things about the gifts he gives that we must have eyes to see. Things about the fruit that perseverance yields. Things about the mending of broken pieces. Things about growth and beauty birthed from difficulty. And after the whispers come the questions: How will we respond to these realities? Will we accept them or will we rail against them, trying so desperately to put our shattered wish-dreams back together? These questions are important to consider, because our response is what makes our friendship *biblical*. Or not.

When Jenny said she'd wrestled with sudden and unwanted bitterness about friendship and the church, she also confessed her gut response: she wanted to run away. She wanted to start over somewhere new with new people and new friendships. But then she realized, she said, that to do so would be like getting divorced and remarried with the illusion that the second marriage would be all that the first wasn't. She wanted to do the easier work of starting over rather than the harder work of digging in, having hard conversations, and taking a good look at herself in order to reengage where she already was. She hadn't felt God releasing her but instead asking her to remain. And she has.

Her response is what makes her friendship biblical: a commitment to continual reengagement with those God has us in relationship with. Reengaging rather than retreating. Reengaging by rooting out bitterness rather than isolating and festering. Reengaging by confessing our hurts and our hurting of others rather than ignoring the problems and letting friendships fade away. Seeking to love and bless no matter the response in return.

All of our wish-dreams are centered on what we hope others will do for us or with us, but biblical friendship considers that all we can truly affect is ourselves. The whispers of God into the realities of our friendships call us to learn from our Friend, who extended friendship first without looking for a return. We are able to learn from how Christ befriends us and, like Abraham and Moses, "friend" others with what we've been given. Biblical friendship treats others as God asks us in his Word to treat them and, at its heart, is a solid trust in him to meet our needs, whether that comes through other people or not. The model we have is one of forward engagement and initiation and very rarely retreat, except for the necessary retreat into our Friend's arms.

Receive Friendship with Thankfulness

Biblical friendship doesn't involve grabbing or clamoring, least of all before God. Instead, at its core is receptive thanksgiving—we receive whatever God has given with gratefulness, placing our hope in him alone.

What does this mean for us?

It means we look around. Our neighbors, co-workers, fellow church-goers, family members—God has placed us in proximity with all of these, and each one is a gift to us. With the wish-dream shattered, we see that Jesus enables us by his Spirit to love and connect with them in the reality of who they are and who we are and in the reality of our daily lives. We can relate to them without weighty expectations or clamoring. We can overlook offenses. We can receive them with thanksgiving and we can do the necessary work of extending ourselves toward them in love.

When we look the realities of friendship full in the face, when we look to God alone for perfect friendship, and when we receive what he gives us through others with gratitude, only then are we able to extend ourselves outward in love in a way that doesn't demand friendship but rather invites it. Only then are we able to partner with God to give and receive the gift of friendship.

Isn't this what we most want and need from one another? We don't need each other's wish-dream standards or expectations; we need safe friendships in which we can breathe and be in process and work things out but also rest peaceably, knowing that our friends will ultimately point us, in our need, back to Jesus.

We don't want the wish-dream. We want friendship as God intended.

And that kind of friendship begins with us.

PART TWO

Threats to Friendship

FIVE

Fear of Being Burned

Perfect love casts out fear.

1 John 4:18

I started popping vitamin D pills today.

It's only September, but it's been gray and chilly for days on end and I can hear winter shuffling around like a kid in his hiding place, ready to jump out and scare the summer out of me.

I'm a Texas girl who's been transplanted to the East Coast. Winter doesn't exist in the part of Texas I come from, just two seasons of hot and hotter. When I was a child, we commemorated Christmas at my aunt's south Texas home by putting on our shorts, so you can imagine how ill prepared I was for my first snow-on-the-ground winter on the East Coast. I didn't own a single pair of boots nor did I have a single practical coat to my name. My poor children took their first sled ride in tennis shoes, their socks hiked up over their jeans to keep the snow out.

Seven winters in, I've learned one important thing: L. L. Bean. I'd been faintly aware of L. L. Bean in my two-season Texas years, but I remember thinking that the L. L. Bean catalog was selling a New England fantasy, not actual, real things that actual, real people used. Like coats and snow boots and mittens.

Now I know that tennis shoes on snow make for nasty falls. Now I know how to tie a scarf. Now I know what to wear when I run errands in the tricky weather combination of rain and wind and cold. Now I know to pop vitamin D pills if the clouds stick around more than a few consecutive days, and they almost always do.

And I also now know that I'm not a big fan of winter.

Except for one thing.

Fires.

I heart fires. I might be willing to admit that I look forward to winter if for no other reason than the delicious fires my delicious husband makes in our delicious fireplace. I love the smell of fires, the crackling sounds they make, and, of course, the warmth they radiate on the coldest of cold days in winter.

Last winter, as a family, we retreated to a mountain cabin not far from our home. After breakfast on our first morning there, the thermometer announced it was 15 degrees outside. Naturally, my kids and husband thought they'd like to go outside in their bathing suits for a dip in the hot tub. I naturally thought I would *not* like to do this, so I let my delicious husband build a delicious fire in the delicious fireplace (while I watched encouragingly), scooted my chair within inches of it, and snuggled up with a cozy blanket and a good book. Every once in a while I'd get up and peek out the window to make sure my family hadn't turned into icicles. On one of my forays away from the fireplace, I noticed that the kids had white patches of frost in their hair and on their eyelashes. I waved, shivered, and went back to my perch by the fire, content to be the only smart one in my family and to enjoy the only good thing about winter.

When Past Hurts Cause Present Fear

What is it about fire? We like to stare at fire, we enjoy food that's been cooked over fire, and we savor how fires make us feel, especially in the dead of winter.

Friendship, in its very best forms, makes us feel as if we're sitting by a raging fire in winter: it touches us at the very core of who we are, bringing warmth and life to cold, weary bones, calling us from the harsh world into the delight of companionship. As a fire is to winter, friends are to life, and life, as C. S. Lewis says, has no better gift to give.[1]

But sometimes fires get out of control. Sometimes, when I'm sitting mere inches from our fireplace, willing the warmth to sink deep into my bones, little sparks snap out at me, stinging my skin or burning tiny holes in my clothes.

Fires can rage. Fires can hurt. Fires can destroy.

As fires go, so goes friendship. Friendship is often the sweetest slice of life, but friendship has also been the source of some of our greatest pain. We've been stung by careless words, ongoing loneliness, the neglect of a friend, snarky gossip, misunderstandings that created unalterable rifts, weighty expectations, the invitation that never came, or a sense of distance from someone we considered a close friend.

It's painful to admit these hurts exist and even more painful to be attentive toward them, because to do so is to rekindle a fire that's raged and burned and left behind scars. But if we want to build fires of friendship that are strong and life-giving, we must first rekindle the hurts that have come before, because these hurts have also formed lingering fear in our minds. And fear is a stubborn impediment to our pursuit of friendship.

We haven't known it was fear. We only know that we tend toward introspection and overanalyzing. We question ourselves and the words that spill out around other women. We apologize profusely. Something has shriveled in the deep, sensitive parts of us, so much so that we want to close in on top of ourselves like a turtle retreating into its protective shell. In internal, imaginary conversations we are angry and accusatory, while our outward demeanor is politely distant. We turn the accusations on ourselves, convinced that everyone feels about us what that one person expressed or, with their actions, seemed to express. We will not give anyone a chance unless they prove themselves, unless they barrel through this brick wall we've erected.

We fear being hurt again.

All of our responses to past hurts are meant to protect us from being hurt again, but they have not served that purpose at all. They have instead fueled the fire of fear, and this is a fire that will never warm us. We don't want the fear any longer but we're also not sure how to let it go. We're not sure how to rekindle the broken friendships we have or, really, our broken thoughts about friendship. But we do want the real thing—the kind of friendship that warms our bones. We just haven't realized how much our own thoughts have worked against us.

Hurts Are Inevitable, Fear Is Not

Friendship begins with a belief, stems from a belief, grows out of a belief. It follows, then, that our thoughts are consequential to our friendships.

If fear lies at the heart of our attempts at friendship, our interactions with other women will be drenched with insecurity. We will be entirely unable to handle conflict, we will lash out at anything that brushes against our old wounds, and we will be quick to retreat at the first whiff of difficulty.

We tell ourselves that this is natural, that this is the way friendship goes.

This may be the way worldly friendship goes, but it doesn't resemble anything we see in Scripture. Fear is an impediment to all the commanded "one another" moments in Scripture, because fear keeps our attention solely focused inward.

I said that friendship begins with a belief. This is the belief that it must begin with: "In this world you will have trouble."[2]

Do you believe those words of Jesus, that in this world you will have trouble? Or do you believe in the fairy tale that says trouble flies away at the sound of Jesus's name? If Jesus is to be believed, and I think he is, everything in our lives will be touched by trouble, including our friendships. We *will* be hurt. Friendship hurts will come to all of us, because friendship is between imperfect people who, no matter how much they seek to honor the Lord in their relationships, will inevitably hurt one another. To bristle at the existence of hurt is to bristle at Jesus's promise. To be surprised and affronted by the existence of hurt is to be surprised and affronted by Jesus. I'm not saying that hurt doesn't hurt; I'm just saying we shouldn't be startled that it happens. As in marriage, the existence of conflict isn't the issue—it's the way we *respond* to conflict that is the issue.

We find friendship difficult because we believe Christian friendship should be all unicorns and rainbows. We tend to believe we're "bad" Christians if we've experienced conflict with others. I would venture to say that the majority of us have only ever encountered unbiblical responses to conflict, so when we experience hurt ourselves, we don't know how to respond other than turning an accusatory finger toward others or toward ourselves.

Friendship, however, blossoms under true belief: "In this world you will have trouble." Yes, now we believe it, but do we believe what Jesus says next? "But take heart! I have overcome the world."[3] Take heart and do not fear, he says, because he has overcome the worldly system that, among other things, teaches that hurt automatically leads to fear and self-protection.

In other words, trouble doesn't fly away at the name of Jesus, but *fear* can. Friendship blossoms under the right belief that we are secure in Christ and that no trouble in this world can snatch us away from his presence, his approval, or his love. This security gives us the ability to march directly into the troubles of this world with an appropriate shield—Jesus himself. He gives us the means to face trouble without fear and come out on the other side having experienced reconciliation and peace.

In fact, facing hurts in friendship and handling conflict biblically can actually grow us in Christlikeness and solidify and deepen our friendships. My friend Susan said this to me once, and I've always remembered it: "It's not a friendship until you hit a rough spot and you have to work through it together." I tend to agree with her and have experienced this firsthand. I value those women who care enough about our friendship to directly address me with their hurts and are willing to listen to mine. That is not to say it's easy or without hand-wringing, but handling hurts biblically always stokes the warm fire of friendship.

It may be helpful for us to look at friendship as the Bible looks at trials. Trials are difficult, but James tells us they are also able to test the genuineness of our faith as we submit ourselves to God in the midst of them. Friendships also are refined, solidified, and deepened when we actually face hurts and work through them rather than turning away in fear.

Let us not forget that the friendship fire we're building is a refining one.

Banish Fear by Committing to Work through Conflict

When I've been hurt by a friend, I've had to take stock of my thoughts. When I'm not sure I want to do friendship anymore or when I want to excuse myself from loving a specific person, I try to stop and take notice of that and ask myself why. If I want to retreat from someone out of annoyance or guilt or because I'm pouting, or if I want to lash out at someone, I'm typically relating to them out of fear. Fear that they won't be to me what I thought they were. Fear of the friendship changing. Fear that they are judging me. Fear that I won't be able to meet their expectations.

Susan can say that friendship is proven through appropriate conflict, because we had some ourselves a few months ago. We were picking our children up from the same location. My husband was out of town, dealing with some difficult personal and ministerial matters, and I'd been emotionally and physically battered by the circumstances. I felt desperate and needy and was (I can see this, looking back) *extremely* sensitive to the words of others. When I saw Susan, I felt a sense of reaching for a lifeline, even for a brief moment. I couldn't have voiced it then but now I can see it: I was looking to Susan to be something for me that only God could be for me in that moment. Susan could encourage me, sure, and she could listen, but she couldn't ease my burden in the way that I really needed.

I shared with her a few details of how I was doing, and her response, which I saw through a tainted lens of self, hurt me. I said, "I can't talk about this right now," did an about-face, got in my car, and drove away.

I felt the opposite of supported and decided to tell her so. I texted her that afternoon to tell her I'd like to talk. She put me off until the next day, obviously hurt herself, although I couldn't for the life of me figure out why.

In those few days, I was a wreck. This gem of a friendship was, I felt acutely, in jeopardy. My fears of losing it, of having possibly hurt her, of having been hurt myself, were loud and throbbing in my head; I could think of nothing else.

But I tempered my fear by turning to the Lord, asking for his wisdom, and resolving to walk directly into the conflict with a heart to listen, to forgive, and to ask for forgiveness if needed.

When we talked, Susan expressed her hurt that I'd not known her heart toward me was one of support and love. I was totally taken aback. I hadn't considered that she would have felt hurt. I hadn't considered what she'd felt as I'd turned tail and run from the conversation. All I'd seen was my own need and my own hurt and all the ways she hadn't been a friend to me, when in fact her response had actually been one of concern and support.

We had a good conversation and we're still good friends, even better than before, I'd say, primarily because we both submitted ourselves to God and to handling our trouble well. We allowed him to point out things in each of us through each other, things like the tricky, sensitive spots we try to protect out of fear and the ways we respond to those unbiblical fears.

And do you see how my thoughts affected our friendship? My thoughts of Susan were not true—she was in fact trying to help and support me. I hadn't given her the benefit of the doubt. I shudder to think of the friendship I'd have lost if I'd allowed my fears to trump my commitment to working through conflict.

I've been hurt. You've been hurt. What are your thoughts about those who have hurt you? Did you have expectations of them that were too weighty? Are you holding on to bitterness even though Scripture tells us to root it out? Are you hurt because you've been keeping score and you feel you're not getting what you deserve? Have you been keeping a record of wrongs? And if you've been legitimately sinned against, are you allowing God to escort you through the process of forgiveness? Are you fearful of being hurt again and therefore unwilling to trust God with your heart?

And, most importantly, do you see what your fears are doing to you and to your friendships?

As Christians, we have only one God-honoring option. We simply don't have the option of not dealing with things or not living in community with other believers. We don't have the option of letting bitterness fester. We don't have the option of staying isolated. In case we ever entertain the idea of a possible loophole, here's what Scripture says:

> Two are better than one,
> Because they have a good reward for their labor.
> For if they fall, one will lift up his companion.
> But woe to him who is alone when he falls,
> For he has no one to help him up. (Eccles. 4:9–10)

> A man who isolates himself seeks his own desire;
> He rages against all wise judgment. (Prov. 18:1)

God says two are better than one. He says that a woman who isolates herself rages against wise judgment. We're intended to live this life alongside others, no matter how we've been hurt in the past or how we'll be hurt in the future. We can only navigate through by giving ourselves to the secure love of God and, instead of letting fear lead to our passivity toward others, letting his love lead to our pursuit of others.

SIX

Ashes of Insecurity

What causes fights and quarrels among you? Don't they come from your desires that battle within you?

James 4:1 NIV

*I*t's hard to look at our hurts, but it's even more difficult to admit that we have at times been the ones who have hurt others.

We've been the ones who, when presented with a candle of friendship, snuffed it out. In our envy of other women and who they are and what they have, we have chosen not to celebrate them or allow them to get close. In our childishness, we've been inconsiderate in thinking that friendship is for us and about us and should be what we want. We've been inwardly critical, and outwardly too, though we might not have dared to address the person directly. We've been judgmental and partial and argumentative and a million other things that sting and divide.

These are ashes of our own making. And though we're prone to stroke and prolong the wounds inflicted upon us, we are not as eager to face the wounds we've inflicted. We want to quickly sweep those ashes aside and pretend they were never there.

I know all too well, because I have ashes of my own making.

They involve my friend Aimee.

I first met Aimee when she and her family moved in across the street. My husband and I had started a church, and Aimee and her family eventually began attending. Her family had moved to our city for her husband's medical training at the local university hospital. She has children of similar ages to my own, and as we got to know each other, we'd often sit outside together while our kids played. We developed a friendship, but somewhere along the way our friendship deteriorated. This is how it happened, from her perspective and from mine.

Aimee: Most mornings I'd see Christine leaving with somewhere to be. She looked put together. She had appointments or errands or coffee dates. I was still in my pj's, herding kids to the table for breakfast and convincing my eldest that subtraction was a good idea. I knew I was called to this life at home, educating my kids, but everyone doubts their calling sometimes. We always have two versions of ourselves competing for our attention. One version of me was the life I was living, and the other version was like the one I saw pulling out of her driveway. Sometimes it was hard to put that other version to rest, because I looked at how I spent my days and at times they seemed so lacking.

Christine: Every day, whether I sat on my couch, opened my garage to leave on an errand, or walked outside to get the mail, I had a clear view of Aimee's house. Sometimes I saw Aimee herself, coming in and out of the house or playing with her children. What I saw was another mom who was making very different choices from mine regarding school for her kids. Aimee is a homeschooling mom, and we were spending more time together during a season when I was surrounded by homeschooling moms, when someone else had told me I was doing the wrong thing by putting my kids in school, and I'd begun to privately wrestle with this specific issue. I wasn't wrestling with it because it was something God was doing in my heart. I was wrestling with it because I feared being seen as less-than, unspiritual, and even blatantly wrong by people I respected. When I looked out the window and saw Aimee's house, I assumed she thought less of me because of my decision. I assumed she thought my kids weren't well behaved or well educated. I assumed a lot of things, but I never voiced them to her, because what if she confirmed them? That felt too risky to me.

Aimee: Christine is an introvert and a writer. She is following a passion she is sure about and has arranged her life in a way that allows her to do it faithfully. At the time, I couldn't be sure if my passions were the right ones and I felt like I couldn't arrange my life at all—I was just reacting to what was thrown at me. She tried to encourage me, but I would go home from our times together and feel like I was drowning. How did she have it all together and I was so hopelessly scattered and undisciplined? Was I lazy or just overwhelmed by my circumstances? Either way, I felt my accomplishments were lacking.

Christine: Aimee is an extrovert. She can spend time with people for hours on end and loves to shower people with her attention and time. I am more of an introvert. I love spending time with people, but I am also drained of energy after spending a large chunk of consecutive time with people.

Almost every time I looked out my window, I'd see a car at Aimee's house, and it usually belonged to someone I knew from church—a younger woman she was mentoring or another homeschooling mom. Sometimes I felt jealous of those relationships. Sometimes I felt I should be doing what she was doing, that she was more effective at ministry than me, the pastor's wife!

Aimee: Most nights I'd hear a car door slam, and if I looked out I could see Christine's dining room light on and know they were eating as a family. I was usually standing at the counter eating oatmeal for the second time in a week. Sometimes after I put my kids to bed I'd look out longingly, hoping to see my husband's car lights announcing his arrival home from the hospital. I'd see the living room light on across the street. I'd ask myself, *What would it be like to be her and not me tonight?* I hadn't heard from my husband all day. I didn't know when or if he would be home. It was the saddest and loneliest time of my life, and I didn't want to admit that I questioned whether my marriage could survive it. Compared to what was happening across the street, I felt that my marriage was definitely lacking.

Christine: I knew how she felt about her marriage because she'd told me. I wanted to protect her from seeing Kyle and me go out on dates or our family spending time together, but I couldn't. Although she never said it, I assumed she thought my husband didn't work hard or that I was an indulged wife who depended too much on my husband. I felt guilty about these things that weren't even true and weren't even said, and I felt I had to prove myself to her somehow—prove that I was working hard, that my husband was working hard, that our life wasn't all roses.

Aimee: She was different from me—different needs, different ways of extending love. I wanted a friend and I knew she wanted one too, so why was this so hard? She was right there, outside my window, and yet at times it seemed like an unfordable river flowed between our two houses. Sometimes I felt like I was chasing her. The invitations seemed one-sided and so did the conversations. She always had so many questions, which made me feel like she was interested in me, but I would walk away unsatisfied because what I really wanted was to know her and I could tell she was holding back. I thought if I just did or said the right thing then maybe she would be the friend to me that I wanted to be to her. My head said that I needed to love her for who she was, but my heart felt insecure and rejected. I didn't know where I stood, and in my dark places that inner voice said over and over, *She doesn't like you.* And then I looked at myself and questioned my value. The answer I gave myself was that I was lacking.

Christine: I was trying to manage a lot in my life, especially this whole pastor's wife thing. I often felt confused at the blurred lines between life and church and ministry and friendships and felt at times like there could be no distinctions. Across the street was a woman who was a friend, a neighbor, a church member, a fellow women's ministry leader, and a person whose pastor was my husband. That was confusing to me at times. Sometimes I tried to talk to her about what life as a pastor's wife was like, but I felt as if I always stumbled over my words and couldn't explain it. I wanted to be understood and listened to, and I knew she wanted me to understand her life as a medical resident's wife, but always in the back of my mind I felt as if I was competing with her to be understood, comparing the issues and difficulties of ministry with the issues and difficulties of being a doctor's wife.

Differences Are Inevitable but Insecurities Are Not

Things in our relationship began to go downhill. It's not hard to figure out why. Aimee was wrestling with her worth and ability and looking partly to me for validation. I was tangled up in assumptions and perceived expectations and not eager to talk about it or do the hard work of untangling.

Her response was to pursue, and my response was to pull away and hope, I suppose, that the issues would magically disappear. She sensed my pulling away and received it as rejection, which wounded her. I sensed her expectation and received it as pressure, which wounded me. We both saw our differences so clearly rather than building our friendship on our commonalities. If we were to sift our relationship in order to account for the threatening thoughts that poured water on the fire of our friendship, they would be comparison, envy, discontentment, worry, and insecurity. The way I thought about her came out in my actions toward her, and none of it was good.

Ashes of our own making.

Even though it's difficult and embarrassing for both of us, it's important to tell our story, because ours is a snippet of what happens all too often among Christian women. We allow broken friendships to drift us apart rather than doing the work of restorative sanctification. Thoughts are allowed to run wild rather than taken captive. Differences are seen as insurmountable obstacles. Wounds are nursed rather than forgiven. And in all of it, we don't want to acknowledge how we're playing a part in hurting or hindering our friendships. We desire the ideal, not the real. We don't like complicated; we like easy. We like it when people like us, are like us, and don't rub up against us like sandpaper, smoothing our rough edges.

If we're going to allow God to sweep away our ashes, we must look honestly at the ways we ourselves destroy the very friendship we long for, and we must allow the light of Scripture to shine into the dark recesses of our minds. Because this destruction typically occurs in our minds. We engage others in our thoughts more often than we engage them with our actions. We enter and leave a room analyzing what was said and who talked with whom. We even lie awake at night recounting relationships, asking:

Do they like me?

Can I make them like me?

Will they accept me?

Will they love me?

What will they give me?

What are they expecting from me?

Will they hurt me?[1]

We harbor insecurities—about our worth, about whether or not we're accepted or "chosen" by others, about what kind of friend we are, about our lifestyle choices, about our personality, or about our spiritual depth. Comparison breeds fearful isolation or eager validation-seeking, neither of which are ingredients for flourishing friendships.

We develop yet simultaneously conceal expectations of others. When our expectations are met, all is well. But when they're unmet? We feel dejected, rejected, unloved, frustrated, and deeply disappointed.

We unleash our harsh inner dialogue, taking off any restraint that keeps our thoughts grounded in truth, leading us to think critical thoughts of ourselves and of others.

We privately crave the attention of certain women we admire. We will also use them to get what we want, perhaps a position or status that will get us where we want to be socially.

We make assumptions about other women based upon their outward appearance, so often categorizing them by how they're different from us. We erect little barriers with these seemingly harmless assumptions. In our minds, assumptions are truth. We don't think to actually get to know the person beyond who we've made them to be in our minds.

We worry that we'll mess up or lose the friendships we do have, causing us to cling tightly to the gifts rather than the gift-giver.

We believe it's better to receive friendship than to give it.

All of these thoughts betray our desires. For security. Validation. Love. Acceptance. Assurance.

For self.

God asks us to lay all that weight of need on him, because laying it on others hurts them and hurts us in turn. He asks us to view one another through a different lens, which we find in 2 Corinthians 5:16–17: "Therefore, from now on, we regard no one according to the flesh. . . . If anyone is in Christ, he is a new creation; old things have passed away; behold, all things have become new."

We're to regard other women not according to their outward appearance or the categories we place people in, such as marital status, life experience, lifestyle choices, or life stage, but rather as fellow new creations. We have the same need (redemption of sin) and the same rescuer (the blood of Jesus), and we serve the same Master. We no longer have categories when it comes to our identity because none of us have, in or through those categories, merited the gift of Christ. We're rallying together around him as the only One who can fundamentally meet our hearts' desires. We're all in process; therefore, we're all on an equal playing field.

As we rally around Christ, we look to one another not for the things only Christ can give but for gifts of edification and sharpening sanctification. We receive the majority of the church's ministry to us through a handful of people—our friends. The very differences we see in others can actually be beautiful gifts to us. When we think about the uniqueness of a friend's calling, it can lead us to worship God. The spiritual gift of a friend that we don't ourselves possess can be a blessing to us when we're in need of that specific ministry. If we will let each individual stand alone as a beautiful new creation of Christ and not lump them together according to secondary identities, we will have an opportunity to worship God instead of comparing and envying other women. It's only in taking this biblical perspective that we can have the true unity and deeper community we hope for. Only then can we be a godly friend to others.

Aimee and I were looking for the other to validate us, not to sanctify us. God had called both of us to our own things (ministry, medicine, homeschooling, public schooling, gifts) that were very different, but he also had called us to each other. He placed us in close proximity to each other. His purpose was for us to learn from each other and be sanctified by each other. When we weren't relating to each other from these truths, we were missing out on the sanctification and edification God had for us.

We were relating to each other according to our secondary identities, not our primary ones, and that is precisely how we hurt each other. That's what happens when we don't live from the truth of the Word. We huddle up according to our secondary identities and we assume others who are different are thinking the worst of us. Or we are privately critical of others in a way that keeps us at a safe distance.

We form circles.

C. S. Lewis calls this the "Inner Ring," where we're drawn to circles for a sense of intimacy. He's not talking about friendship and natural affiliations. He's talking about our selfish desires to be "in" with those we want validation from. He says, "Unless you take measures to prevent it, this desire is going to be one of the chief motives of your life."[2] Our desire for insular friendship leads us to ask ourselves the wrong questions: *What can I get from this person? How can I categorize this person? What will this person do for me?* But the Friend leads us to ask, *How can I serve this person? How can I bless this person? What can I learn from this person?*

We like circles because they make us feel secure. We can exclude people who make us feel uncomfortable. We can refuse to hear different perspectives or confront the idea that we might need to change. However, we may be excluding the very voices God wants to use to help us grow and wounding them in the process.

Christine: After several months of a deteriorating friendship, Aimee asked if we could talk. I went to her house and she bared her soul, telling me how she felt confused and hurt by my pulling away from her. I confess that I was cold toward her even in that conversation. I just didn't want to work at the relationship at that point, and I was unwilling to truly look at the wrong I'd done to her. I think I was also unwilling to be honest with her about how I felt hurt. I just wanted to be done with the relationship, which only served to hurt her more.

Aimee: After another few months, Christine emailed me one day and asked if I had anything else I wanted to share with her. She wanted to continue our previous conversation. I was pretty surprised by this. I'd spent those dormant months trying to move past what had happened to our friendship, all while we were living and ministering in close proximity to each other. It was really difficult, but God used those months to work on my heart. Because I had no recourse to work through things with Christine in person, I had to work them out with the Lord. I had to ask his forgiveness for the things I had done that prompted what happened to our friendship, and I had to ask him to help me forgive her for the ways she had hurt me. I had worked through things with God vertically, but when she wanted to talk again, I wondered if God was giving me the opportunity to work through things horizontally as well. When we spoke again, the barriers were broken immediately. I believe the reason is that God had prepared Christine's heart to hear and my heart to love, both things we had struggled with in the past. I don't think I could have said yes to that conversation had I not had that vertical transaction with God, where I was willing to sort out the process of forgiveness without any promise of closure. That experience prepared me for what ended up being a truly God-appointed and anointed conversation.

Christine (in a follow-up email): I've thought more and more about what has gone on in my heart that would have caused me to respond to you the way I did. I feel like I was blind to a lot of things about myself, and God's conviction has helped me see some things that I just didn't see for a long time. There is a lot of change that he needs to do in my heart, especially dealing with that lie I shared with you, that I believe I'm a disappointment. It's become a way of thinking for me this year and it's been very destructive. I appreciate your willingness to forgive after so much. God is good.

Aimee (in response): I appreciate what God has done in me through this process too. My issues have also come to the surface and it has been a painful process, and I'm better for it. Better for having known you, even if some of that time hurt. So I'm going to say to you something that is hard for me to say. That, in the end, I want what I've always wanted, which is to be your friend. It is hard to say because it is putting myself out there again. I feel fine and am fully satisfied with where we left things. But I'm saying it because I think you need to hear that even with everything that happened, I *still* want to be your friend.

Aimee and I had a conversation. We offered confession, repentance, and forgiveness to each other. But that's not the end of the story. The end of the story is that we built on that conversation. We came to a resolution and made a commitment to take something hard and allow God to make it something beautiful. We wouldn't relate to each other from our differences; we would relate to each other from our commonality as new creations in Christ.

SEVEN

Kindling for the Campfire

We lament that we have no staunch and faithful friend, when we have really not expended the love which produces such. We want to reap where we have not sown. . . . The secret of friendship is just the secret of all spiritual blessing. The way to get is to give.

Hugh Black[1]

So here we are, committed to sweeping away ashes in order that we might build fires of friendship. Starting a fire takes skill and nuance—at least that's what I've learned from watching *Survivor*.

At home, I stuff months-old newspaper under a grate that's propping up my chopped wood, strike a match, hold said match to the newspaper, and—*voila!*—a fire appears and I am instantly, gratifyingly warmed.

But on *Survivor* they are not allowed human dignity in the form of properly sized clothing, three square meals a day, or matches. Fire-starting on TV takes muscle, sweat, and the grueling, painful rubbing of sticks against a hollow chunk of bamboo.

Everyone on *Survivor* is extremely focused on getting fire because it's essential for boiling water (subsequently used to wash the tribe's dirty underwear), but everyone *really* cares when a fire-starting contest is the

69

tiebreaker that determines who will go home. Game on. Each alliance hopes their representative fire-starter has actually paid attention when fires have been started back at camp, but generally those put forward through the vote are patsies with no clue as to how they should use the flint, coconut husks, and their own breath to form a proper fire.

I prefer fireplace fires to *Survivor* fires, probably because I prefer coziness and food and not wearing my bathing suit on national television. Or I should say I prefer sitting by my cozy fire and eating cupcakes while watching people who are starving try to survive in the wild for my entertainment.

But as I was saying, I notice that fire-building takes nuance and skill, and—I think this is perhaps most important—it takes the proper kindling. No matter what island the survivors are stranded on, when they want to build a fire they always look first for coconut husks, bamboo sticks, and small twigs. Do you know what else I notice? The contestants spend an inordinate amount of time seeking these things, because without kindling they have no fire and without fire they can't survive. The kindling doesn't magically appear at the campsite; they have to seek their own survival.

Be a Kindling-Seeker

There are, however, always one or two in the *Survivor* bunch who perpetually laze around at the campsite, expecting others to do the work for them. These contestants cannot seem to see what everyone else clearly sees: that they are reaping rewards from work they've not done and they inevitably will get their comeuppance. They will suffer because of their lack of effort.

Sometimes we are that blind about ourselves in our friendships. Friendship requires an inordinate amount of seeking and gathering kindling, but our own self-preoccupation often leads us to passivity. If we're really honest with ourselves, we feel as entitled as the lazy survivors. We much prefer for others to do the seeking and the gathering and all the backbreaking work to get the fires of friendship going; we're fine sitting around and waiting for the reward. Whether from self-consciousness or laziness, we simply don't want to have to take the initiative with other women—but we also have no qualms about grumbling when we lack a fire to warm us in the night. Self-preoccupation that hinders initiation is, simply put, a major hindrance to friendship.

Instead, we should want to be seekers. Initiative-takers. Kindling-gathering fire-builders.

If we were to observe a strong Christian friendship, we could always work our way backward and find that it is between two people who seek the good of the other rather than being preoccupied with themselves. Their thoughts are not primarily turned inward but outward. They take the initiative to serve, gather, and bless each other. They seek and gather necessary kindling.

What exactly is the kindling so vital to friendship that they seek and gather?

They Seek and Know the Love of Christ

"He who is of a merry heart has a continual feast" (Prov. 15:15).

A merry heart has little to do with personality or gifts of hospitality or trying to conjure up a certain feeling. In fact, a merry heart is not an external practice but rather an internal joy. A woman who knows Christ's finished work on the cross cannot help but be a joyful and free person. She sees that she is loved by God and that nothing can separate her from that love. She is secure in his approval, safe to reveal herself to God and allow his work in her heart. Because of this, the snare of craving approval and validation from others is loosed, and she discovers that she can approach others without weighty, idolatrous expectations but rather with love and service and delight. God satisfies the longings of the heart, making friendship a beautiful gift to enjoy.

They Seek Fellowship with Others

"They devoted themselves to the apostles' teaching and to fellowship, to the breaking of bread and to prayer" (Acts 2:42 NIV).

We are, in the shadow of the first disciples, encouraged to be *devoted* to God's gifts of community, fellowship, growing and learning alongside others, and enjoying God together. In other words, we have an example from the first disciples of godly friendship in which people are prioritized over tasks, activities, and passive, thing-centric entertainment. Godly friendship doesn't usually develop through convenience; it develops through devotion. Convenience doesn't anchor us when we get annoyed with someone or the circle we're in includes someone we don't have a natural affinity toward. Devotion does. Convenience doesn't mesh with the burdens and time constraints of daily life. Devotion does. Their experience wasn't an emotional, experiential wish-dream. Friendship was for the disciples as it is for us: a choice and a devoted commitment, one requiring perseverance.

They Seek to Be Generous

"Whoever brings blessing will be enriched, and one who waters will himself be watered" (Prov. 11:25 ESV).

When it comes to friendship, even if we're seeking and knowing the love of Christ and placing a high value on friendship, we can still go wrong if we simply sit back and wait for others to come and be a friend to us.

The basis of cultivating biblical friendship is generosity—*showing* that we value others and seeking to be a friend. Paul says it like this: "Let nothing be done through selfish ambition or conceit, but in lowliness of mind let each esteem others better than himself. Let each of you look out not only for his own interests, but also for the interests of others" (Phil. 2:3–4).

An important kindling for a blazing fire of friendship is God-compelled generosity. He himself has given us the model. Jesus summarized his mission in this way: "the Son of Man did not come to be served, but to serve" (Matt. 20:28). Paul referenced Christ saying, "It is more blessed to give than to receive" (Acts 20:35).

Do we believe this? I tend to be much more preoccupied with myself and with what others are doing for me or whether or not they're extending friendship in my direction. Scripture nudges me from passively waiting to actively doing—loving, serving, blessing, and encouraging.

This state of mind is so essential to cultivating new friendships. We are called to be initiators—we won't wait for what we want in a friend but instead will go out and be that friend for others. A generous initiator attunes herself to the needs of others and looks for ways to meet them. Biblical friendship is active rather than passive.

We don't do these things so that we will be watered, in the analogy of Proverbs 11:25, or because we think this will guarantee that others will do the same for us. We do these things because the act of doing them honors God and others and waters our own souls in the process.

They Seek the Best in Others

"The merciful man does good for his own soul" (Prov. 11:17).

How do you think of others? Through what filters do you sift their responses (or lack thereof)? Do you tend to think the best or the worst of others? Do you tend to think that they are thinking the best or the worst of you? How we think about others matters.

Recently, a friend told me that someone she has been close to had not been returning her texts and phone calls. My friend had been reaching out and reaching out, but her efforts hadn't been reciprocated. She felt hurt by her friend and, as I saw it, she had two options in how she could respond. She could assume the worst of her friend, be hurt more deeply by the apparent rejection, stop reaching out to her, and let cracks form in their friendship. Or she could assume the best of her friend—perhaps there were things going on in her life my friend wasn't aware of, or the stresses of life were preventing her from good communication. She could give her the benefit of the doubt, perhaps a little space too, and, if the lack of communication continued, she could broach the subject directly with her friend.

In order to enjoy biblical friendships, it's important that we actively seek to think the best of others and also assume that they're thinking the best of us, unless they give us concrete evidence otherwise. Being a merciful person creates a safe environment for friendship to deepen and grow.

They Seek to Know Others

"A fool has no delight in understanding, but in expressing his own heart," and "Good understanding gains favor" (Prov. 18:2; 13:15).

No human being is a simple, linear creature. We are all complex, we all walk a hard road, and we all have stories for days about our fall and redemption. None of us are without our joys and our struggles, and each of us is deeply loved by the God who created us in his image.

In other words, every person is fascinating.

It's hard to remember that when we look at hard exteriors or at those who appear to have it all together and who we assume couldn't possibly understand what we're walking through. It's also hard to remember that about people we put on pedestals or those we honestly find annoying or hard to relate to.

The Bible tells us, however, that a wise person seeks understanding of others and allows this understanding to evolve into compassion. In fact, seeking understanding of others is a way to invite friendship because, as we understand others, we naturally become a more gracious and empathetic person. In the eyes of others, an understanding person is a favorable choice for a godly friend.

How do we gain understanding of others? It's actually quite simple: we ask questions and then we listen to the answers. Unfortunately, many people, including Christians, don't make a practice of asking good questions and actively listening to others. They just want to talk and be heard. Or they don't think to ask questions that might enable them to know another woman beyond their shoddily built assumptions of her. Perhaps they see other people as a service provider: "I talk and you listen; now I feel better."

As a pastor's wife, I have a front-row seat to our difficulty in this area. I regularly have long conversations in which I'm not asked a single question. I hear from women in our church who are discipling younger women, and these young women want to talk and share but do not consider asking any questions of the older, wiser women sitting across the table from them. It seems we want to express ourselves fully and are offended when others don't listen or care, but we don't consider what we can learn from others.

The Bible tells us this is what a fool does, and common sense tells us that a lack of understanding drives people away. People who seek to understand through questions and listening? These are the wise ones, and they invite friendship.

Most of All, Cultivate a Faithful Heart

I love camping. Minus packing up half my house, sleeping on the hard ground, constantly swatting bugs, and making the half-mile trek in the middle of the night to the restroom that smells like animal.

Yep, camping minus the actual camping is awesome, mainly because of the campfire. Until nightfall, camping is all sweat and mosquitoes and searching for cell service and properly confining food in order to keep bears (BEARS!) from snuggling up to you in your tent.

But when night falls? The cooking fire grows up into a *campfire*—less utilitarian and more dazzling and fun. The darkness temporarily hides all the bears peeping at you, the bugs crawling on you at that very moment, and the reminders that you're going to be tossing and turning on the dirt in the middle of nowhere in a few hours. In that darkness, the campfire provides the only light—a beautiful, flickering light—and all campers gather around it, daringly close to the flames, to warm themselves, set marshmallows alight, or simply stare into it. There is something about a campfire that seems hypnotic or mesmerizing. It also provides a sense of intimacy and togetherness. Stories are told, thoughts are shared, quiet moments are allowed. Faces are hazy, but all eyes are all-the-time glued to the campfire, basking in its warmth and pull.

The campfire is a perfect picture of our goal of tossing our old embers of fear and bitterness and taking the initiative to gather the kindling of generosity and understanding. We're attempting to make something with our lives that exemplifies faithfulness to God, which is more important than making friends or deepening friendships. The goal, ultimately, is faithfulness rather than friendship, but our faithfulness to God is evidenced by how we love others, and this love of others inevitably attracts people. Friendship is a happy by-product of faithfulness.

C. S. Lewis basically tells us to quit sitting around, preoccupied with whether others will befriend us, and to instead purposefully seek to live a (faithful) life:

> The very condition of having Friends is that we should want something else besides Friends. Where the truthful answer to the question *Do you see the same truth?* would be "I see nothing and I don't care about the truth; I only want a Friend," no Friendship can arise—though Affection of course may. There would be nothing for the Friendship to be *about*; and Friendship must be about something, even if it were only an enthusiasm for dominoes or white mice. Those who have nothing can share nothing; those who are going nowhere can have no fellow-travelers.[2]

In other words, cultivate a faithful heart. A faithful, generous heart is interesting and attractive. When you focus on faithfulness to the Lord, you may be surprised who gathers around your fire and whose fire you find yourself around. The categories and criteria we like to place on others and on friendship tend to fall away.

When we moved from Texas to Virginia and I got my friendship do-over, the first thing I did was drop the categories and criteria. I put my kindling together by resisting self-preoccupation and focusing instead on living a life of faithful obedience. There were awkward and uncomfortable times when I wondered if anyone would gather around my fire or if I'd be invited to gather around another's. I felt unsure of myself and even wondered if I knew how to make friends any longer. But then it happened: after time blew into my small flame, I found others standing around in the dark, staring into my campfire. They saw what I saw. They wanted what I wanted in life. They had the same doubts and fears and struggles of the heart as I did, and the same desire to live a life of faith. But they were also different from me in all the ways I'd previously categorized women. It was only in laying those categories aside that I began to develop deep and true friendships.

Sometimes I still feel a sense of building my fire and wondering if women are there, staring into the flames with me. I've come to terms with the fact that friendship is not static but rather ever changing just as people—including myself—are ever changing. At times I feel insecure and lonely, mostly because I'm getting all tangled up looking at myself, but every time I get in that place, I feel the Lord's nudge to take the criteria blinders off and look around at the women he's placed in my life.

There are always others around. We may not know them intimately yet, and we may be scared to try to get to know them. We may know them somewhat, and we know that what it's going to take to go deeper is probably going to be uncomfortable and even risky. We may be too quick with the categories and criteria, turning them away before they even have a chance. But they are there.

EIGHT

The Spark

If we walk in the light as He is in the light, we have fellowship with one another.

1 John 1:7

She's been coming to our church for several years now, but I don't know her well. I've talked with her several times, trying to draw out more than one-word answers, digging for a subject that makes her come alive, but I still don't know her beyond what her résumé might tell. I think I make her nervous, or maybe it's that I'm overbearing, so I try to give her space.

In her, I see myself, the woman I've been before who was anchored by self-consciousness. She's private and reserved but she continually shows up, hoping to connect. I wonder if her internal monologue resembles my old one: *Who will care for my kids if I get sick? Who will I call if something tragic happens in my life? Who can I let my guard down with? Who do I really know, and who really knows me?*

I invite her to our women's retreat, not because I'm the pastor's wife and am filling some quota, not because I'm teaching and want a huge crowd, and not because it's something to talk about when I see her at church. I invite her because I see that look in her eye: the look of being an outsider, the look of isolation, the look of being contentedly closed off but also deathly afraid to stay that way. I invite her because I want to know her and I want others to know her.

She says no. She says it with absolute, total conviction, a no that feels like it's answering all future invitations, a no that indicates it's not busyness keeping her away, a no begging for explanation. So I gently probe. She describes past experiences of women's events characterized by shallow conversation, girly crafts, and topics never veering far from marriage and motherhood. I tell her what we're studying (not marriage or motherhood) and guarantee there will be no girly crafts but rather lots of opportunities to make connections with other women. She thanks me for the invitation, reaffirms her no, and moves off into the crowd coming into church.

As she goes, I am sad, not for me but for her and for the "us" that is our church's women, because we're not going to know her until she lets us know her, and we're probably missing something wonderful.

But I am also sad because I understand where she's coming from. I understand what it's like to walk into church with a smile but also a heavy weight of insecurity and to overanalyze everything I've said after it's all over. I understand what it's like to get all twisted up in paranoia about friendships and to wonder if I've said too much after sharing something personal. I understand the pressure to appear put together and the pull toward assumptions and comparison. I, too, question myself, fear getting it wrong, and want connections beyond surface conversation. I wish I could help her see that, even though I'm the pastor's wife and often out front, we have more in common than she thinks.

As she walks away, I pray that she will someday discover the secret spark of friendship, the secret that starts the fire.

Ignite the Fire of Friendship

There are as many ways to ignite a friendship as there are types of friendship, and most involve commonalities and proximity—mommy friends, church friends, work friends, online friends. We hope beyond hope that our deepest friendships will develop through commonalities and proximity alone. But sometimes they don't. We can put all of our kindling together and hope for the best, but there is something else needed. What is the spark needed to ignite that fire of friendship?

It's vulnerability.

Vulnerability happens when we reveal ourselves—our thoughts, feelings, stories, homes, families, and struggles—to others. Vulnerability happens when we trust others with the sensitive areas of our lives, those aspects about us that feel fragile or reveal our imperfections. Sometimes it even feels vulnerable to extend an invitation or ask a probing question of someone we've only known on the surface.

Vulnerability feels risky because it involves embracing weakness and imperfection. Image-keeping feels far less risky because we believe it protects our sensitive areas from the judgment of others. For some reason, we believe impressing other women will lead to connection and community, so we expend effort on building an image rather than revealing ourselves. But until we lay down our defenses, until we stop trying to shield our insecurities and shame from the eyes of others, we will not experience the friendship that goes beyond the surface level, the kind we so long for. An unwillingness to be vulnerable is a threat to deep friendship.

Do you want to know a secret? People can see through our defenses anyway. We're not hiding as much as we think.

Vulnerability is the way we lay down our arms. Vulnerability takes a weakness and makes it a strength, a bonding agent, because acknowledging our need for God and others attracts fellow vulnerable sojourners like a magnet. Perfection-striving may impress from a distance, but it is vulnerability that wins friends.

When we share with others that we have a need, a struggle, a doubt, or an uncertainty, we also invite God's power into our lives. The Bible says that God's power is made perfect in our weakness, so wouldn't it be safe to say that we experience God's power alongside others when we share those weaknesses? A godly friend is one who embraces us in our weakness, listens to our uncertainty, and then points us to God, but we can only give and receive this ministry when vulnerability pervades the atmosphere between us and our friends.

If we want to spark a fire of friendship, we *have* to ask for help and invite others in.

I'm not talking about constantly gushing out our every emotion to everyone we meet. I'm talking about nudging new friendships deeper by having women in our lives in an informal way. I'm talking about sharing our sin and how God has redeemed it. I'm talking about asking a friend to watch our kids so we can go to marriage counseling. I'm talking about calling a friend when we're having a bad day and asking them to pray for us. I'm talking about being the first one in our small group to share a deeply personal prayer request. I'm talking about letting safe people see us cry. I'm talking about confessing sin to a godly friend. I'm talking about letting people into the private areas of our lives, both our physical spaces and our emotional and spiritual spaces. I'm talking about asking for help when we're in over our heads.

Vulnerability is the spark we need.

The Risk and Reward of Vulnerability

Biblical friendship is grounded in vulnerability, because vulnerability is necessary to fulfill the "one anothers" found in Scripture. Galatians 6:2 says, "Bear one another's burdens, and so fulfill the law of Christ." The word translated *burden* implies a load too heavy for one person to carry. How else can we help carry a load unless we know the load is there? How else can someone help us carry a load unless they know what we're trying to carry? The same can be said for the other "one anothers": confess your sin to one another, love one another, instruct one another, serve one another, bear with one another, forgive one another, spur on one another, and pray for one another. All require vulnerability.

Vulnerability is risky, yes, but in biblical friendship the Holy Spirit guards our vulnerability. We aren't to value vulnerability more than we value the Lord and his wisdom; to value vulnerability and "realness" above God leads us to spew every thought and emotion and to idolize ourselves and other people. We must filter everything we share with others through the leadership and help of the Holy Spirit. As we walk by the Spirit in our friendships, he will help us know when to share and when we need to hold back and rely solely on the Lord to meet our needs.

As I've been writing this chapter, in fact, I've been convicted by the Holy Spirit that I at times value the help of others more than I value the help of the Holy Spirit when I have needs. Even as I was convicted of my idolatry of self and others, my instinctual response was to call my closest friends to talk about it. I knew the heart of my desire to be vulnerable was to seek comfort and counsel from people rather than from the Lord, and the Holy Spirit both held me back and turned my heart toward the care offered by my Father.

Wise vulnerability is actually less risky, because it keeps the Lord between us and our friends and it doesn't require another person to be our Christ. Wise vulnerability allows us to seek the Lord with others and gives us the opportunity to remind one another of the hope and redemption we have in Christ. Wise vulnerability invites and even asks for pointed biblical truth in response to our sharing.

One of the most interesting and exciting things God does in and through our vulnerability is to show us our heart-level commonalities with other women. When we don't want to take the risk of vulnerability, it's often because we assume that those we engage with in life couldn't possibly understand our situation. A married woman assumes that of an acquaintance who is single. A young mom struggling with postpartum depression assumes she's the only one in her church fighting despair. A woman hiding a secret, shameful sin assumes that if other women knew they would be horrified and reject her. A young woman assumes that an older woman couldn't relate to her insecurities.

But when we're willing to take the risk, we soon discover that every single one of us has something in common: *need*. We are, all of us, sinners, and we are, every single one, in need of the same salvation and sanctification. God gives us all the same rescue—Christ—because although we face different challenges, our heart issues are strikingly similar.

Wise Vulnerability Helps Us Grow

My friend Sarah, as we got to know each other, kept saying to me, "There are things about my life that, if you knew, you wouldn't be my friend anymore."

I said, "That's not true. There's nothing you've done that God hasn't forgiven, and if God has forgiven, who am I to hold it against you? Plus, bringing shameful things into the light negates the power they have when we keep them secret."

She said, "Don't be so sure."

She knew the truth of God's grace toward her, but she also had an internal monologue going that constantly shamed her and questioned the extent of God's forgiveness. Eventually, she told me those secret things, which she'd never told anyone. And everything changed in our friendship according to her vulnerability. I had the incredible privilege of listening to her long-held secrets and the even greater privilege of negating her inner monologue with the truth of God's grace.

Something else happened: her vulnerability sparked a process of God's healing, and she started telling other women about her sin and subsequent redemption. And we, because Sarah had talked so openly to us, began talking to each other about her palpable example of God's power to forgive and heal and about the hope of the gospel for our lives too. We all marveled and rejoiced! We were seeing the gospel tangibly at work.

One woman said to me, "I grew up in a church where we *never* talked about personal things. We talked about behaviors and right and wrong, but we didn't talk about what happens when everything has fallen apart."

I can relate. I, too, for many years saw Christianity through the lens of behavior and outward appearance. I didn't understand the depths of my sin, which means I also didn't understand the depths of God's grace. I hadn't seen an example of the power of the gospel applied to a dark, shameful situation and the redemption and healing that can result. So when I struggled, I felt like a deficient Christian and hid it from others.

Wise vulnerability opens our eyes to the depths of sin in our lives and the lives of others, but it's also an invitation to see the Lord at work in the darkest of places. It's through vulnerability that we discover the grace we can rest our hope fully upon. We recognize that the gospel of Jesus is strong and powerful and has something to say to us in our darkest places.

Perfection doesn't exist, even in our churches. Everyone needs a safe haven from the world where perfect behavior and outward appearance are not mandated in order to be loved. That safe haven is God's power working through our vulnerability as we walk alongside one another in friendship.

Remember how I said I didn't have friends for that long season in my life? Well, I was wrong. I had potential friends. I just hadn't lit the spark of vulnerability in the kindling of those friendships, because the risk of revealing my insecurities, uncertainty, and imperfect self seemed too great.

Our Commonalities

At the retreat—the one I invited the woman at my church to attend—I stood before the women who gathered and, even as the words tumbled out, I wanted to take them back. "I don't always like women's events." I actually said it. *The pastor's wife at a women's event said she doesn't always like women's events!*

"Because I get nervous," I continued. "Because there is this pull to compare and a fear of revealing ourselves, and I have all these insecurities." The room got still. "Raise your hand if you're nervous too. Raise your hand if it was hard to come this morning." Hands slowly went up all around. "So let's just drop all that, and let's get down to it. Let's not pretend with each other. Let's give and receive. Let's share and learn. Let's love each other well today." The room released an audible sigh, and we got to work studying and discussing Scripture together.

Later, when I had a moment to think, I immediately berated myself for saying such a vulnerable and stupid thing. But then, one by one, women whom I know and love approached me and told me of their own insecurities about relating to other women, about their appearance, about not knowing the answers, about sharing their struggles and doubts, about not having it all together.

They understood from my words that I would understand. *We have more in common than we think.* Saying it out loud just did something for us all, because we women tend to think about and assume our differences more than our commonalities. And our differences, as seen through the filter of insecurity, could only drive us away from one another.

I saw that day what helps us push through our fears and insecurities and awkwardness and come together: *naming.* Naming our common struggle and our common need is what helps us get to the true friendship we crave, and with true community comes true growth. *Because where we name common need, we can also name common grace in Christ and grasp him together.*

I wish she had been there, the woman from church. It might have felt uncomfortable and awkward for her at first, but she would have found herself among fledgling friends expressing common needs and receiving common grace. I'll invite her again next time, and maybe I'll tell her that I don't always like women's events either, that I get nervous about them even as the pastor's wife. Maybe she won't believe how much need we have in common, but I'll speak to her of common grace all the same and invite her into the community waiting for her on the other side of insecurity.

For her, the vulnerability needed will be simply showing up.

"Christine Hoover opens the door and welcomes us all to richer, deeper, and more meaningful relationships in *Messy Beautiful Friendship*. She writes with wisdom, understanding, vulnerability, and profound insight as she unpacks the brokenness and beauty of relationships among women. This book is a must-read for anyone hoping to build healthy and God-centered friendships in their lives."

Melissa Kruger, author of *Envy of Eve* and *Walking with God in the Season of Motherhood*

"Christine truthfully voices what so many of us feel about friendship, that it's harder than we expect and yet more needed than we sometimes admit. This book inspires us toward more meaningful friendships and a deeper understanding of the God who brings us together. I'm personally grateful for Christine's gentle and helpful exhortation . . . so applicable and timely."

Ruth Chou Simons, author and artist; founder of GraceLaced.com

"Everyone who is a friend or who desires meaningful friendships should read this book! As one who has struggled with the messiness and beauty of finding and maintaining friendships, I found this book so helpful. At points, Christine's stories echo my own—the fumbles, the assumptions, the 'hashtag friends,' the unmet needs and joys. I've longed for the illusive ideal of friendships that serve me and squeeze God out of my life rather than embracing the divine reality that my friendships are opportunities to love the Lord with all my heart in fellowship with others who are doing the same. All that we think we want and need from a flourishing friendship can be found in Christ. He is whom we should seek and long to be in friendship with, and by his amazing grace, he gives us friends who are dim but beautiful reflections of his friendship with us."

Kristie Anyabwile, pastor's wife, mom, writer/speaker

"Few things in life can match the beauty, warmth, and consolation of a true friendship. Similarly, few things in life can be as disappointing, distressing, and disillusioning as a friendship gone bad. Christine Hoover acts as an able guide on a journey to discover what the Bible has to say about friendship. She kindly leads the way, humbly guiding us through the Word of God to unveil a vision that is truly worth pursuing in every way. Do yourself a favor: grab a copy, read it, digest it—then go find a friend, walk through the pages together, and find yourselves at the other end more wholly prepared for your final home."

Jonathan Holmes, pastor of counseling, Parkside Church; author of *The Company We Keep: In Search of Biblical Friendship*

"Friends . . . we take them for granted when we have them. We miss them when they're gone. We're hesitant about new ones, and we're scared to go deeper with the ones we have. Christine Hoover has written a book about friendship that will minister to you no matter what season of life you are in and no matter what your current perspective on friendship may be. This is possible because she draws from the timeless truth of God's Word and points us to Jesus, our Savior who has befriended us."

Gloria Furman, author of *Missional Motherhood*
and *Alive in Him*

"Christine Hoover not only uncovers the roots beneath the frustration, disappointment, and loneliness we often experience in our pursuit of friendship but also sets us on a clear course toward discovering and nurturing gratifying, intimate, God-designed friendships with our fellow sisters. Filled with biblical wisdom, practical advice, and compelling personal stories, *Messy Beautiful Friendship* reminds us exactly why friendship is a gift from God and how we can give and receive it with grace, gratitude, and joy."

Michelle DeRusha, author of *Katharina and Martin Luther: The Radical
Marriage of a Runaway Nun and a Renegade Monk*

"Doesn't every friendship just 'happen' like it did in elementary school when your neighbor was your best friend with whom you shared a seat on the bus and passed notes in class? Thirty-some years later, I need this book. Christine Hoover, with refreshing approachability and lightness, approaches a loaded topic from God's perspective. *Finally,* here is a timely word to women, using his Word as guidance, on how to do this crazy thing called friendship *well*."

Sara Hagerty, author of *Every Bitter Thing Is Sweet*

"Every person will one day find themselves in a season where friendships are messy, difficult, or nonexistent, and in those seasons it can be tempting to blame-shift, check-out, or declare it too difficult to be sustained. Christine Hoover has written a book for all of us who find ourselves where we do not want to be and never envisioned we would be. *Messy Beautiful Friendship* is a book on how to be a friend and how to make them, how to keep them and how to keep from worshiping them. This is a book for every woman who has said to me, 'I feel so alone,' including myself. Christine, in an act of friendship toward her readers, makes us laugh, listen, and see ourselves on every page and challenges us to see Christ as our greatest joy-bringing relationship."

Lore Ferguson Wilbert, author and speaker

PART THREE

Discovering and Deepening Friendship

NINE

Be Kevin Bacon

Take Initiative

Let us love one another, for love comes from God.

1 John 4:7 NIV

*I*f I could encapsulate my middle school years into one word, without question it would be *awkward*.

I was a middle schooler in the late '80s, which means I was basically an awkward person at an awkward stage inside an awkward decade. A sandwich, if you will, of awkwardness. I had the requisite sky-high '80s bangs, shellacked so heavily with White Rain hairspray I could move them as one solid piece. I also sported a perm, tight-rolled jeans, and two pairs of colored socks tucked inside my white Keds. My favorite shirt had an inexplicably huge peacock painted across the entire front. My look was completed by braces and such a large quantity of rubber bands in said braces that I couldn't open my mouth at all and was forced to talk through clenched teeth. To eat my bagged lunch, I first had to spend five minutes removing those colored rubber bands.

Why, in this awkward stage of life, do we also have to endure social activities that exacerbate our insecurities? It's like middle school exists solely to taunt us.

My middle school had an inordinate amount of school dances, which I both highly anticipated (because boys) and greatly feared (because boys). These dances were held in the gym, and it was always an unsettling feeling to be walking around the school at night without textbooks to hide behind. My friends and I would enter the gym in a compact, giggling herd—a pack of animals protecting themselves against the common predators of isolation and insecurity.

When it comes to school dances, *Footloose* was no lie, except for the part when Kevin Bacon, who's been practicing punching and kicking the air in an empty warehouse, shows up and everyone suddenly becomes fantastic dancers and instinctively knows the choreography. Middle school dances are perpetually the beginning of that final scene in *Footloose*, where the guys and girls are on separate sides, no one dares talk to the opposite gender, the music is lame, and absolutely no one knows how to dance so they just stand against the wall trying to look casually cool. Everyone's waiting for someone else to make the first move.

That's certainly what I did. On the fast songs, I left my perch on the bleachers to lurch around in somewhat of a dancing movement. I tried to laugh and giggle a lot in the circle of dancing girls because I wanted to appear confident and interesting. Mainly, I wanted to attract the attention of a seventh-grade boy—*any* seventh-grade boy.

However, my plan never seemed to work. I was never asked to dance. After many middle school dances where I was not chosen, and lots of bleacher thinking time, I got an idea: *I* would be the one to cross the great gender barrier and ask a friend from one of my classes to dance! Just once, just to prove to myself that I wasn't awkward after all. Just to prove to myself that I could be on the inside for once. And also, I wanted to make good use of my totally awesome peacock shirt.

So I did it. After one of the fast dances ended, when the boys started for one side of the bleachers and the girls for another, before I could talk myself out of it, I did the unthinkable and asked a classmate to dance.

He stared at me for an eternal millisecond and then said, "Sure." We shuffled back and forth awkwardly, as distant from each other as we possibly could be and still be considered dancing together—definitely leaving room for the Holy Spirit. We didn't speak a single word to each other; we only stared over each other's shoulders as the song wound down. But inside I was nervously giggling. I felt victorious, not because I believed I'd won the love of a middle school boy, because I definitely didn't, but because I'd silenced my insecurities and actually experienced an actual dance at the school dance.

That must have been what Kevin Bacon felt when he arrived with his date and kick-started an otherwise lame dance. He didn't care what anyone thought and he didn't wait for anyone else to take control. No way. He's the guy who's not afraid to kick off his Sunday shoes and cut loose. *Footloose.*

Discomfort Needed

Making friends and even deepening the friendships we already have feels eerily similar to being an awkward middle schooler at the dance. We show up. We put our best foot forward. We want to be invited and chosen because we want so badly to belong. We gravitate toward the huddle of people just like us. It all feels desperately awkward and clunky as we hang out against the wall, hoping for someone—*anyone*—to make the first move.

Really, we're all just separated by an unwillingness to be uncomfortable. It's too uncomfortable to cross the floor. It's too uncomfortable to strike up a conversation with someone who appears as foreign as a middle school girl does to a middle school boy. It's too uncomfortable to reveal our lurching dance moves when no one else is dancing under the glaring strobe lights.

I am one of the most awkward people I know. I'm actually quite shy, I'm hopeless at telling a good story or delivering the punch line well, and I tend to ask penetrating personal questions way too soon after meeting someone. Basically, I'm still the same girl who chose the peacock shirt for my stint on the bleachers, except I've thankfully shed my braces and rubber bands.

I'm an expert at being awkward.

And I have realized I'm not the only one who feels awkward in relationships. Everyone is uncomfortable. And everyone wants to be loved. Which means that anyone who is willing to resist and push through the discomfort has an incredible opportunity to make friends.

I learned this through church planting, because when you start a church in a city where you don't know a soul, and when you have a three-year financial deadline to form a self-sustaining church that has actual people, you figure out how to push through awkwardness and meet people pretty quickly. I was crossing dance floors right and left—chatting up moms at the park, inviting strangers into my home, joining the PTO, and interacting with anyone who so much as glanced in my direction. Little ol' shy, nerdy me. And guess what? People responded. They chatted back, they accepted my invitations, they were happy to have me volunteer. *People are waiting for someone to care.*

Sometimes, if you want to know the truth, it *was* awkward. They'd ask why we'd moved to town and I'd tell them about the church we were starting in our living room—and they'd get quiet and stare off into the distance, unsure what to make of me and silently willing me to go away.

I learned to just keep at it, because I had started connecting with women and getting to know them and, wouldn't you know, actually making friends. Making these connections had little to do with my personality or my marital status or the ages of my children. It had everything to do with my newfound willingness to push through my own discomfort and initiate with others over and over and over again.

Push Through the Awkward

We are women who long for community and to live lives of purpose, but just like anything else that is good and beautiful and worth having, these things don't come just because we want them. The secret to discovering friends is to be a person who is willing to bust in like Kevin

Bacon, ignore the gasps and the silence, see a person who wants to be known and loved underneath the casual cool, and move toward them. In other words, be someone who isn't afraid to take the first step, look a little silly, and possibly be rejected or misunderstood. Someone who isn't afraid to push through the awkward.

In order to be a friend and have friends, we have to get over ourselves and just go for it. Invite an acquaintance to coffee. Visit a small group in your church even though you won't know anyone and *give it time and effort* before you decide whether it's working or not. Ask an older woman whom you admire to get together. Start a book club in your neighborhood even though it's possible no one will show up. Serve alongside others. Ask penetrating questions to turn the conversation onto spiritual things. Confess sin to someone you consider a friend. Host a game night and invite people you want to get to know. Say yes to an invitation from a co-worker even though you've never spent time together outside of work. Basically, do things that make you feel uncomfortable but will possibly invite deeper friendship.

Of course, it's true that we may push through the awkward and then things will be, well, *awkward*. The person may not respond how we hoped she would. She may not get why we're doing what we're doing. Our expectations and hopes for friendship may take a little tumble. We may have to do the work of getting ourselves back up and dusting ourselves off.

But it's also true that we may push through the awkward and experience all sorts of incredible things, like a freeing dependence on the Lord and a new or deepening friendship.

We simply can't know unless we go for it.

Just like Kevin Bacon.

TEN

Back Doors

Open Your Home and Heart

Offer hospitality to one another.

1 Peter 4:9 NIV

I've always wanted back-door friends, and I've known that they aren't easily made, but I haven't always known how to get them. Perhaps you've wondered the same. How do we move from first greetings and initial awkward conversations to full-fledged, back-door friendship? It helps, of course, if we're committed to pushing through the awkward and being initiative-takers, as we've already discovered. But there is something else we all have at our disposal, a surefire tool for discovering and deepening friendship: our homes. If we want back-door friends, as in the back door of our *homes*, it follows that we will need to regularly invite people into them.

Having other women in my home was terrifying to me for many years. Welcoming someone into my private space felt (and still feels) vulnerable, as if I'm welcoming them into everything that makes me, me. Also, I am a recovering perfectionist, so I spent wasted years fretting over elaborate meals and decor and how I'd make everything impeccable despite the small children underfoot. The what-ifs plagued me. *What if they say no to my invitation? And what if they come only out of obligation? And what if the food is undercooked? And what if I'm not an interesting conversationalist? And what if they think my house is too small or my furniture is outdated? And what if their kids spill ice cream on the carpet?*

I let the what-ifs play on the loudest volume in my mind, until one day I decided the what-ifs weren't as important to me as making friends. I wanted friends more than I wanted to try to impress people. My home and my table were readily available tools for forging friendship that I'd completely neglected.

Imperfect Hospitality

We all tend to do this. We have the thought, *It would be nice to get to know her more. Maybe I should invite her over.* But something stands between the first thought and the second. Something causes us to hesitate and to shrink back. Something keeps us from asking.

Perhaps we have misconceptions about what hospitality is. Perhaps we define it according to a worldly standard, where hospitality can only happen when we finally get our home to look like a Pottery Barn catalog and perfect a menu from *Bon Appétit*. If all cannot be done immaculately, we believe it's not worth doing at all. So we don't ask, because we live in an apartment and there are Goldfish smashed into the carpet and we have only one bathroom and what would they think?

Or perhaps we just use the perfectionist ideal of hospitality as an excuse. Perhaps the real issue is that we're afraid to ask because what if she doesn't want to be friends? What if she thinks we're weird? Asking someone to get together sometimes feels very vulnerable and risky. So we don't ask, because of ourselves and this notion of having to be perfect.

Then there are other things that cause us to hesitate (or maybe it's just me). I make assumptions about people. *They wouldn't want to.*

They're too busy. They are in a different life stage, and I don't know what to do with that. From what I know, we probably wouldn't have anything in common. Most assumptions, however, are far from true. They typically only serve to create further divisions between myself and others and fuel my insecurities.

It might help to return to a basic definition of *hospitality*. The New Testament word means "love for outsiders." There is nothing in there about place mats or centerpieces, nothing about receiving a return invitation, nothing about hanging out with only certain types of people. It seems to imply a strong pursuit, a seeking of those who are outsiders to invite them to become insiders.

There are many things that set Christians apart from their surrounding culture. Not all of these differences are welcomed by our culture, but there is one that both sets us apart and is received by the culture as refreshing: hospitality.

Hospitality breaks through the multilayered barriers that Western culture erects: physical barriers that keep us apart, almost hibernating in our homes; emotional barriers of isolation, individualism, independence, and loneliness; and spiritual barriers that make us avoid any heartfelt conversation or disclosure of needs. Hospitality, if done well, promotes physical togetherness, relationships, and spiritual community.

Hospitality, then, is our joy and opportunity. By inviting people into our homes and our hearts, we depict our own spiritual aliveness and togetherness—where we once were alienated from God, now we are reconciled; where once our relationships were broken by sin, now they have been made whole by grace and forgiveness. Hospitality practiced by Christ-followers displays the gospel.

I am amazed at the reactions I get when I invite women I have just met into our home: surprise, delight, gratefulness. One woman said, "I have lived here for many years, and my family has never been invited into someone else's home." This saddens me, but it also displays the powerful opportunity we have as believers to impact lives through simple meals and warm conversation.

Be a Back-Door Friend

Hospitality is not reserved for outsiders only. It also strengthens the church and invites friendship. When women tell me of their loneliness, I discover they are rarely initiating fellowship with anyone. They are living as if they are alienated when in reality they aren't and don't have to be.

I'm not saying these things because I am a joyful hostess at all times, because I have all the right decor, or because I am a gourmet cook. I say these things because I have discovered that hospitality is a simple way of blessing others, a simple way of kick-starting relationships, and, probably more than any other thing, a tool for deepening friendships. Consistent, imperfect hospitality leads to back-door friends.

Imperfect is the key word. We're inviting other women into the realness of life, not into a *House Beautiful* magazine. We're inviting them into relationships—to know and be known—not into an event or a formal presentation.

In other words, if we want back-door friends, we have to *be* a back-door friend. Front doors are generally the Martha Stewart of doors: painted bright colors, decorated with beautiful wreaths, and flanked by potted plants. Front doors are our best foot forward. Back doors are not usually spruced up at all. In fact, they're often plain and unassuming. Mine is in disrepair and has boy fingerprints smudged all over it.

Being a back-door friend means we let other women see our disrepair and smudges, without apology. We don't present ourselves as polished— we don't *present* ourselves at all, really. By being a back-door friend, we simply invite people to be themselves, because we are ourselves.

We can only take up this definition of hospitality when we are free from our worldly confines of front-door image-building. We can only take up this definition when we know and want to live out the gospel.

The gospel takes away all excuses, all assumptions, all self-focus. Second Corinthians 5:14–15 says that the love of Christ compels us outward and, as Tim Keller describes, enables us to experience the freedom of self-forgetfulness. True hospitality is birthed from self-forgetfulness.

So we must wipe away the worldly idea of hospitality. Love is not built between people through beautiful decor or ornate meals. Love is built when we turn our eyes from ourselves and are compelled outward, when our attention and thoughts are toward others and making them feel welcomed and loved.

When we think of it that way, the possibilities suddenly appear endless: hospitality can happen at church, at the mailbox with a neighbor, at the playground, at the grocery store checkout, at work, and even within our own families. How can we bless our neighbor in our conversation with them? How can we celebrate our children? How can we serve those we interact with at church through our words and actions? How can we invite and include?

Hospitality is not a checklist, a try-harder kind of thing. It is a matter of the heart, a posture toward others that draws friends to become back-door friends.

So let's be done with excuses. Let's put to death those silly insecurities. When we think of inviting someone into our homes and our hearts, let's ask her.

It may just be the Holy Spirit leading.

And she just might say yes.

ELEVEN

No Makeup

Share Your Story

Blessed be the God and Father of our Lord Jesus Christ, the Father of mercies and God of all comfort, who comforts us in all our tribulation, that we may be able to comfort those who are in any trouble.

2 Corinthians 1:3–4

Where I come from, a woman doesn't dare go to the grocery store or even to the mailbox without wearing her makeup. To be seen without makeup is a social ordeal leading to profuse apology ("Oh, honey, I'm so embarrassed. I know I look just *awful!*") and myriad excuses given by the one who would *dare* enter the public arena with an unmasked face. The brave makeup-less ones are often met with bless-your-heart questions regarding illness or tiredness, because clearly something cannot be right.

When we moved from Texas to the East Coast, I immediately noticed the lack of makeup on the faces of women passing me on the street. I also noticed their lack of eye contact as we passed shoulder-to-shoulder and their irritated side-eye at my happy hello and neighborly head nod or wave. But I was mostly struck by the naked faces. I felt subconsciously overdressed and very Texan, simply because I was wearing lip gloss.

After my initial discomfort at being culturally "different," I settled nicely into a routine of minimal makeup, although I haven't given it up entirely and never will, because that'd be like giving up my roots altogether. However, there is a sense of freedom in not being made up all the time, of going to the grocery store without makeup, and of ultimately feeling that there isn't an appearance I have to maintain. I kind of like it when people see me without makeup; there is a sense of being purposefully authentic, of not covering up the blemishes or the bags under my eyes that betray my age. I no longer feel as if I need to apologize when I'm not perfectly put together. And, happily for me, there are no bless-your-heart questions to accompany my sloppiness.

I once knew a woman who wouldn't let her husband see her without makeup. Because she rose earlier than he did each morning in order to put on her makeup and fix her hair, she'd almost become a living legend other women discussed with a little awe and a whole lot of fascination. To accomplish such a feat would take so much planning and so little precious sleep that it raised the question: *Why on earth?*

However much we want to judge that, why on earth do we similarly hide ourselves from other women under protective barriers of shallow conversation or busyness or isolation? Why do we cover over our true thoughts, struggles, and feelings in order to protect ourselves? Why do we feel we have to impress other women? Why are we so afraid of one another?

Why on earth?

This is what I see underneath all of our protective barriers: stories. Stories of deep need and sin, stories so secret that we've been shamed into utter silence, stories that are in progress, stories that have made us into the people we are, and stories that have concluded in profound redemption.

These stories are the good, rich stuff of who we are and where we've been.

However, just as going without makeup in Texas feels risky to me, I think these are the very stories that take guts to share. It's quite possible that our greatest fears—of rejection and judgment—may come true when we share these stories.

But what if our stories are God-redeemed precisely so they will be shared? What if they are our greatest tools in not only extending and inviting friendship but also extending and inviting others into the comfort and the grace of God?

What Is Your Story?

God has given me multiple stories and, as I've shared them, I've found them to be beneficial not only for increasing my faith in him but also for increasing others' faith in him.

I wrestled with legalism for many years and felt all the emotions that are birthed from attempts at self-justification: pride, condemnation, burdensome living, guilt, and shame. When God rescued me from myself and taught me about his true gospel, I suddenly had eyes to see the countless women in my life struggling under a similar burden. My entry into their lives hinged on me sharing my story, and as I began to share, God brought more and more of these women to me, and me to them. My story became my ministry.

In addition, for many years I struggled to forgive people who had deeply wounded me. Anytime I heard a sermon on forgiveness, the Lord would bring a certain person to my mind and I'd immediately shut off. Frankly, forgiveness felt impossible. I almost cherished the wounds and enjoyed recounting how I'd been hurt. However, in time, I submitted to the conviction of God and began purposefully working to forgive each time a memory surfaced. I learned that God is a God who sees and that I can leave conviction and discipline of others up to him. I read the parable of the unforgiving servant (Matt. 18:21–35) and recognized the absurdity of my unforgiveness. Learning to forgive became a part of my story and, as I shared it, this part of my story also became a bridge toward others.

I also have a child with special needs. When he was diagnosed, there was one woman in particular who entered into my suffering by sharing her story with me. She brought me comfort by pointing me to Christ, and in him I found hope for parenting. This, in turn, became a part of my own story, one I have shared numerous times with other moms. It's never an easy story to share, because doing so is like touching a wound that has never fully healed. The story comes out in quiet moments and with carefully chosen words, but it's ultimately a story of viral hope and supernatural comfort. My story, because I've been willing to share it, has sparked and deepened friendships with other moms who can relate.

Some of my best stories stem from my husband being a pastor. My greatest sanctification has come from being a pastors' wife. For many years, I didn't talk about pastor's wife things with anyone; they felt too fragile to release from my protection. In other words, I felt inadequate and I didn't want anyone to know. Many pastors' wives feel this way—which I discovered when I started talking and writing about my own experiences and wrestling. This part of my story has been an additional bridge to friendship with other pastors' wives and even with other women in our church.

Even more than I've ever potentially blessed others, I have learned from my friends' stories. My life and faith have been profoundly enriched and expanded from hearing and seeing how friends have faithfully approached suffering, a husband's infidelity, death of loved ones, sexual sin, marriage to an unbeliever, chronic pain, and depression. I'm grateful they've entrusted those stories to me, because through them I have been assured that God is real and his gospel is powerful. I have grown in my faith and we have grown in our friendships.

What is your story? Your experience with infertility or being adopted or sexual abuse or learning to love Scripture or moving or being a military wife or marriage difficulties or being a working mom or singleness—any or all of these have hopefully been a marker of God's grace and comfort in your life. They are not completely closed wounds; healing and redemption are never quite as black-and-white as we make them out to be, and sometimes it's in the sharing and receiving of words that we gain new perspectives that help us grow. But these things can also be a bridge. God has likely placed someone in earshot who needs to hear your story. And perhaps he's also placed that someone there to be your friend.

Reveal Yourself

It may seem silly to compare going without makeup in public to sharing some of the most intimate parts of ourselves with others, but they both take a conscious decision to reveal ourselves. All of our stories have some level of sin or difficulty or brokenness at their core. Most of our stories are not stories we would have chosen for ourselves, which often elicits shame. Our stories are sensitive; to share them requires our authenticity and vulnerability. But when we sit across the table from another woman and share our stories in appropriate moments, it speaks of hope in Christ and gives her permission to share her own stories. Honestly, those moments are a sigh of relief in a relationship. They invite us to go without makeup with each other, so to speak, and that freedom is like pouring fuel on a warm fire. It breathes life into a friendship. Walls immediately fall away, because everyone is attracted to authenticity and vulnerability, and everyone longs for a friendship where they can wrestle openly with the realities of life without also being offered pat answers or clichéd counsel.

We don't have to be afraid. Remember, we're perpetually safe to share ourselves with others because we're hidden in God's love forever. If we're in Christ, nothing can separate us from his love. In fact, it is this very love that propels us outward to share our stories so that the comfort we've received can also be a comfort to others.

This is biblical truth put into practice.

> Blessed be the God and Father of our Lord Jesus Christ, the Father of mercies and God of all comfort, *who comforts us* in all our tribulation, that *we may be able to comfort those who are in any trouble*, with the comfort with which we ourselves are comforted by God. For as the sufferings of Christ abound in us, so our consolation

also abounds through Christ. Now if we are afflicted, it is for your consolation and salvation, which is effective for enduring the same sufferings which we also suffer. Or if we are comforted, it is for your consolation and salvation. And our hope for you is steadfast, because we know that as you are partakers of the sufferings, so also you will partake of the consolation. (2 Cor. 1:3–7, emphasis added)

Paul's words warn as well as support us. We aren't to reveal ourselves for the same reasons worldly women do. We don't use our stories to manipulate, shock, celebrate sin, or bring attention to ourselves. We use our stories as bridges to others in order that we may encourage, exhort, speak truth, help, invite God's healing, and press others toward righteousness and running their race in honor of God. We offer an otherworldly hope, and in that offering we often discover a beautiful, biblical friendship.

So, my sister, tell what God has done in your past and, with your most intimate friends, tell what he is doing presently as you're working out your salvation. Tell of God's faithfulness and redemption. Tell of what you're most afraid to say out loud, because your sister has a word of truth and grace God has given her that she can give to you.

Make it a point to go without your makeup. Tell your stories.

TWELVE

Dance Card

Make Space for Friendship

In a busy culture like ours, all our other loves will push themselves upon us. Friendship takes incredibly deliberate time.

Tim Keller[1]

I wouldn't mind living in a Jane Austen novel. When Emma Thompson realizes Hugh Grant isn't yet married in the final scenes of *Sense and Sensibility*? His self-conscious hat-wringing and her stifled excitement get me every time, although in general it's less the ubiquitous unrequited love that I enjoy and more the dresses, sprawling estates, and intricate dances.

Apparently we get the phrase "I'll pencil you in" from the dance card days. Using the pencil dangling from her dance card, a proper lady kept track of what partner she'd agreed to for each listed dance. When her card was filled, she'd politely decline any newcomers. She'd say, "Nah, I'm good," and curtsy. Or something like that. I need to figure that part out before I start my life in a Jane Austen novel, because I intend to have a consistently full dance card.

I will certainly be able to call on what I've learned in my regular, non–Jane Austen life, because regular life can sometimes feel like an overflowing dance card. We're constantly "penciling in" (or in my case "Google calendaring in") responsibilities, demands, necessities, tasks, activities, and priorities. As a mom of growing kids, I'm holding not only my own dance card but also the birthday party, field trip, and playdate dance cards for all of my children. I'm often double-booking dances, choreographing drop-offs and pick-ups, and running frantic and frazzled from one commitment to another. The life dance isn't often slow and enjoyable; it usually involves lots of sprinting and sweating.

So when we're presented with opportunities for friendship—we meet someone who's new to the community or a longtime friend pitches a get-together—we're often tempted to look at our dance card, sigh, and conclude it's too crowded. We're too full for friendship. I mean, where does friendship fit on a dance card that includes work, children, a significant other, ministry commitments, extended family, and the routine tasks of feeding and watering people? We barely have time to see the friends we've already made, much less make new ones. Throw in physical distance, varied seasons of life, new babies, caring for aging parents, and the limits of being a finite human being, and where could friendship possibly fit on this overflowing dance card?

This is actually a topic I've wrestled with lately. I had one of those freak-out moments when I wondered who my friends are, and God convicted me that I was placing a high value on friendship in my mind but not in my schedule. Time with friends usually gets stuffed into the random holes in my schedule, but because my dance card had been *too* full, there had rarely been any holes to fill. One of my friends, when I talked to her about it, gently said, "I know that you value your friends, but time with us sometimes seems like a last gasp when you're really feeling run-down." Ouch. It was obvious that I needed to reconsider my dance card and *why* it was often too full for friendship.

Save a Spot

When dance cards were at their height, women often practiced "dating ahead." In other words,

> young women began filling out their dance cards in advance of the evening, to ensure that they would not be without a partner. Many women worried about not being asked to dance, as the most beautiful, best dancers were constantly engaged on the dance floor; the women without partners were often looked down on and pitied. Young women feared not having a partner for every dance, and having a dance card allowed them to make sure they would be busy dancing the entire night.[2]

I admit that when my dance card becomes overly full, it's typically because I too am fearful. I don't want gaping holes, because gaping holes might indicate my lack—lack of productivity, lack of meaningful activity, lack of relationships, lack of purposefulness, lack of being chosen. An overly full dance card keeps me on the move, and being on the move means I don't have to stop and think too much. It's less risky to be always on the move than it is to say no to activity, to choose relationships over being productive, or to be still and quiet.

What friendship needs, however, is time—time for unrushed conversation, good listening, and harmless fun. Friendship doesn't need lip service; it needs attention. So we must purposefully keep spots open on our dance cards. We might need to say no to various wonderful activities or that extra hour of sleep or peripheral things. If we want friendship, we need to make decisions that align with that priority, such as taking the initiative to get friends together, spending the necessary money to visit a long-distance friend, planning in advance or being bravely spontaneous, dropping everything for a friend in crisis, shooting a text or dropping a card in the mail, penciling phone dates on the calendar, intentionally seeking out that interesting newbie in our neighborhood for conversation at the playground, letting the kids watch an extra video or two while we have coffee with a friend, or inviting that fellow homeschooling mom and all her kids over even though it means getting behind in school and possibly incurring a messy house.

In other words, we have to do what we have to do. Because in the end, it'll be worth all the extra effort.

Do What You Have to Do

When I graduated from college, my friends and I started a yearly tradition of gathering for a weekend at the end of July. We didn't put much thought into it at first. In fact, I'm not sure we intended it to be a yearly tradition, but after a few summers of gathering together at the lake, it became just that. We developed traditions within the tradition: floating the Comal River, eating good food, taking a group photo, and completing a marathon share time—we now incorporate a stopwatch, although it is generally disregarded—in which everyone gives a life update. Erin, who is both our unofficial secretary and our official photographer, records it all for those who have to miss. We've seen each other through difficult diagnoses, marriage hardships, unwanted singleness, widowhood, death of parents, struggles with work/life balance, and moves. We've celebrated marriages, babies, milestone birthdays, new jobs—and now we're discussing parenting teenagers and getting older.

That sounds ideal, doesn't it, to have a group of friends like that? It does sound ideal on paper, and in fact that group of girls is a tremendous blessing in my life, but you know what? I live thousands of miles away from where we gather, as have multiple women in our group over the years. It costs us all money and time and effort to get there. Some of us have to find babysitters for the weekend or take time off from work. And not only that, but I've changed from the girl I was when we graduated from college, as has everyone else. In some ways, our differences now are greater than our commonalities. Our closest friends are the ones we spend our every-days with, not the girls we see once a year, and, honestly, it would be fairly easy to quit making the trek to see them every July.

But these are friends who've seen me through over twenty years of life. They are priorities to me, because I know that if I went off the deep end, they would come running after me and attempt to resuscitate my faith. If Kyle and I were struggling, they would champion my marriage. If I were in need, they would be there. That's what we do for each other.

I have to keep a spot open on my dance card for these friendships (and others) that I so value. I have to be willing to make the sacrifices it takes to have these friendships. I have to do what I have to do.

In everyday life, that looks like getting up early for breakfast with a friend and making it back home before my husband goes to work. That means talking on the phone with a long-distance friend even though talking on the phone is not my favorite thing to do. That means going to women's ministry events at my church. That means planning walks with friends on Sunday afternoons. That means inviting friends over for dinner. That means a quick text when a friend pops into my mind.

Everything in our culture works against friendship. We move at such a rapid pace and live such over-scheduled lives. Whereas marriage, work, and family are permanent commitments, friendship is a voluntary commitment and is therefore easy to neglect. If we're going to leave room on our dance cards for friendship, we're going to have to be firmly committed to it and to going against the grain of our culture.

Cut Some Slack

One of the things I also have to do, however, is cut myself some slack. There are some years I can't make it back for our girls' weekend in July. There are some months when my dance card is full because God has purposefully filled it and I don't have the time I'd like for life-giving friendships. There are times when we're all going to be limited by circumstances, and in those times we have to trust the Lord with our limitations and with our friendships. We have to, as my friend Amy says, surrender to what we wish was happening.

And you know what? We also have to be quick to cut our friends slack. Sometimes *they* are limited in time and capacity. Sometimes, no matter how much effort is put into getting together, they just can't make it work. Sometimes they have very little to give. Friendship is never going to be perfect, but that's not a reason to give up our pursuit of others. As we continue investing our time into friendships, we will find that the treasure of having faithful friends far outweighs what it costs us in time and effort.

I have to do what I have to do.

And so do you.

THIRTEEN

Friend Magnet

Honor Others

Be kindly affectionate to one another with brotherly love, in honor giving preference to one another.

Romans 12:10

*P*erhaps you're one of those people with friends coming out the wazoo. I am friends with people like you. You are likable, fun, considerate, helpful, and all-around good human beings. You are awesome. I flock to you.

These friends of mine, upon hearing that I was writing a book on friendship, asked me to tackle these questions: How does one foster intimate, true friendships and remain hospitable without becoming cliquish? Is it even healthy to cut off the number of friendships you have?

The friends that I mention are women using their influence to serve others, honor others, seek out the best interest of others, and love others in a way that brings glory to the Lord. For those of you who are jealous of the friend magnets in your midst, to be fair, I don't think it's as cut-and-dried as it seems. I believe these women are a real-life chicken/egg scenario: Do people *come* toward friend magnets simply because of who they are, or do these friend magnets consistently *go* toward others ready to bless and honor? I see my friend-magnet friends working hard at friendship and being extremely others-centered. They are genuinely interested in others, honor others, and listen to others. My friend-magnet friends all have wildly different personalities, so it's not that they have a charisma, necessarily, although I think they are delightful people. They are simply people who consistently go toward others, no matter who they are, and seek to make other women feel comfortable.

Keep an Eye Out

If you are a person who attracts friends easily, please know that you've been given a gift from the Lord. You've been granted a magnetism and a way of making people feel loved. Thank him for this gift, but please also recognize that this gift is not about you. You've been given the gift of influence, and it's important to consider how you will use it.

In fact, if you are a woman who attracts friends easily, you probably aren't even reading this book. But if you are, my encouragement to you is to use your influence to serve the outsiders. Keep an eye out for the marginalized, the fringe, the new, the lonely, the quiet and unsure ones. Your influence pointed in the direction of an outsider can have great impact. It doesn't take much—a word of welcome, an invitation to a playdate, a thoughtful encouragement about a job well done, or remembering her name—and a whole new world opens up for the one who needs a world, any world, to open up.

A sweet friend of mine from church just moved away to a different state this past summer. She wrote and told me of the loneliness and uncertainty she's feeling, especially in her efforts to connect within a local church. This is a woman who loves the Lord and, while mothering young children, sacrificially served in our church. She is eager not only to connect but also to serve where God has taken her. She wrote what she wished others could see:

It is the first day of Bible study. I am in a new town and have had a hard time making new friends. I have looked forward to today, to an opportunity to meet some sisters in Christ, hoping to find My People in the midst of a storm. Please make me feel welcome.

I come to the steps of the church. I have a child on each side and a stroller. You all say hello, then watch as I try to lift the stroller up the stairs. Please help me.

I am in a new place. I don't know where to go and don't see any signs for where to bring my children. Please direct me.

After dropping off my children, I meekly walk back toward the main entrance. I don't see any signs directing me where to go. Good! There are some moms behind me! I will wait for them, smile, and ask if I can go with them. I try to make eye contact. They continue with their laughter and conversation and walk around me. Please just say hello.

I finally find the sanctuary, yet I don't feel safe. I see all these sisters in Christ. But they all seem to know each other and are not interested—or at least don't seem to be interested—in making a new friend. Please help me find a place.

I bow my head and pray. I ask the Lord for the strength to get through the morning and that I will now respond to others the way I wish someone had responded to me. Please, Lord, let me feel your presence when I feel so alone. Let me find my place at your feet.

I see a friend, the one person who has reached out. She smiles and makes room. Thank you for being like Christ and showing love.

There You Are

My friend needed to simply be seen by someone who could pull her in, and she finally was. The person who pulled her in was a woman looking out for others rather than herself. And she is likely a friend magnet.

The truth of the matter is that we *all* have the ability to be friend magnets when we enter a room with the words, intentions, and body language of seeing others—*There you are!*—rather than saying *Here I am! Everyone look at me! Everyone listen to me!* or the opposite, false humility response, *I hope no one notices me. I will feel too self-conscious.* We esteem others as more important than ourselves. We keep an eye out for the one standing on the fringe of the circle. We move toward the outside and pull those we find there into the mix. And let's face it: Don't we all feel like we live on the fringes in some capacity? Haven't we all felt like an outsider at some point? We all know the relief of having someone pull us from the outside to the inside. We'll be their friends for life.

Make Connections

An honoring person who looks for the outsider soon becomes a safe person for many, many women. In other words, her opportunities for friendship are abundant and overflowing. This is why my friend-magnet friends are asking, "How does one foster intimate, true friendships and remain hospitable without becoming cliquish?" and "Is it even healthy to cut off the number of friendships you have?" Because a person who honors others will eventually have to navigate these things.

And I say, in response, that part of honoring others is *connecting* others. There is a special kind of joy in connecting two women we think will hit it off or who share a story, interest, or life circumstance. We don't have to be everyone's bestie, and just because we've included someone doesn't mean we have to become their intimate friend. We can help foster community among women by being a bridge between them.

So, for my darling friends who are worried about having too many BFFs to handle, this is what I would say: honor all and be deep friends with some. Be friendly and hospitable to all and give intimate attention to a few. Welcome all. Keep an eye out for all. Love all. You don't have to be close friends with everyone, but you can certainly use your God-given influence to bless others and connect women with one another. Be a friend magnet and you'll attract joy too.

FOURTEEN

Naming

Know Who Your People Are

The righteous should choose his friends carefully.

Proverbs 12:26

Sometimes I forget who my friends are. Once, it came out of me like a wail lobbed in my husband's direction: "I've been thinking [read: emoting] for the past five minutes, and I've come to the very scientific and rational conclusion that I don't have friends anymore!" (Pause for garbled crying and pitiful nose blowing.) "No one likes me, obviously, because right in this moment of my greatest need, although I've not told anyone except you that it's my moment of greatest need, no one is here to validate me as a person."

Or something like that.

Kyle interjected to name all the wonderful women in my life and to remind me that I spent time with said women as recently as the night before.

"That was last night! This is now. Relationships change, you know." (Pause forlornly in order to grab a fresh tissue.)

Despite all evidence to the contrary detailed by my husband, at times like this I am *absolutely convinced* that my relationships have suddenly evaporated or, if I'm really feeling all the feelings, that they've never existed in the first place.

I've learned—after riding far too many emotional roller coasters—simply to name. Well, OK, I've learned to first check my monthly calendar. But then I name.

I literally get out my journal and write names in the margins. The names I write are my friends—the women I'd call or text if I needed something, those I'd ask out for coffee just because, those I'm drawn to and enjoy, and even those I'm interested in getting to know better. I don't ask permission to write their names in my journal. I don't call them up beforehand and say, "Are we friends? Can I write your name in my journal?" They don't even know I've written their names down, which is probably well and good, because they might consider it kind of creepy. I don't write them down in order to feel better about myself; I simply write them down to *remember*.

Naming gives me pause to consider if I'm pursuing my people and giving attention and priority to my friendships. Naming causes me to reflect on my relationships and, in turn, to thank God for them—both the burgeoning friendships and the deepening ones.

I think most of us don't necessarily feel like we've got all our friendship ducks in a row. Unless I'm a weirdo, which is highly possible, I think we all tend to have moments when we think, *Just who are my friends?* In my humble opinion, I think this occasional question can actually be a sign of doing relationships right rather than wrong. If we can't point to any relationships at all, that's certainly an issue; but when we have various relationships in various stages of development across different life stages or in different locations or from different circles, it can sometimes feel like we are doing it wrong because we don't have a BFF or a tight-knit circle of friends. That seems to be what everyone envisions and everyone wants, but if we're a Jesus-loving, others-minded person, we're likely going to have many different types of relationships spread across multiple circles and, therefore, we may not always be sure who our friends are. There will be occasions when we need to privately name our people.

My friend Marylyn is that kind of person. She lives with roommates who are also her friends. She disciples younger women. She purposefully seeks out the company of women from different life stages. She is intentional about visiting her college friends, all of whom live out of state. She maintains relationships with friends who have moved away. She also serves faithfully in our church. But she told me recently that she doesn't have a best friend and that she was sort of sad about it. I can see where she's coming from and I get it, but I also look at her life and am astounded at how faithfully she loves and serves so many people. She has her foot in multiple circles and she's a blessing in all of them. She's doing everything right. She just might need to name every once in a while and *remember*.

Name Your People

Who are your people? If you don't know, consider these questions:

Who is your greatest friend? (Hint: Sunday school answer. Always, it is our God, the only One who can possibly see you and know you intimately in all ways.)

Who are the women in your life you enjoy spending time with?

Who are the women in your life who encourage your faith?

Who are the women who leave you feeling like life has been breathed back into you when you're deflated?

Who are the women God is nudging you toward and giving you an affinity for?

Who are the women you want to learn from?

Who are the women God might be asking you to invest in as a mentor?

Who are the women God is seeking for salvation and wants to use you to minister to?

Write their names down.

When naming, it's a biblical imperative that we choose our *closest* friends wisely. We shouldn't allow just anyone to have access to our deepest thoughts and emotions, because with access comes influence.

Proverbs 22:24–25 gives one of many warnings found in Scripture: "Make no friendship with an angry man, and with a furious man do not go, lest you learn his ways and set a snare for your soul."

Similarly, Proverbs 25:19 says, "Confidence in an unfaithful man in time of trouble is like a bad tooth and a foot out of joint."

Solomon warns in these verses (and others) that we shouldn't name as close friends those people who are consistently angry, unfaithful, manipulatively dramatic, gossipers, and conflict-stirrers, because they will influence us in ways we don't want or need. Instead, we should name those who are consistently seeking God and will encourage us to do the same. These are friends who will enter into our adversity with true hope and faithful witness. These are friends who will offer gentle and loving correction as the Holy Spirit directs them. These are friends who will hold our words in confidence and pray for us. These are friends who give us life.

To me, that is one of the most important markers of close friendship. When I name, I name people who I enjoy spending time with, who I leave feeling filled up by rather than drained by, and who push me toward the Lord in the ways they live and serve and speak. Not everyone God calls me to fits these criteria, but my closest friends always do.

Look back at your list. Are you investing wisely when it comes to friendship? Are your people—the people you're giving your most revealing thoughts and moments to—challenging you, helping you grow, and pointing you to Christ? Are you pursuing those whom God wants you to pursue?

Naming is not the same thing as favoritism or exclusivism; we never want to use naming as a fence to keep people out. Rather, naming is simply a marker for stewardship. *What relationships are priorities for me in this season of life, and how can I invest well in those? Am I stewarding well the friendships God has given me?* We are limited people and can't spin infinite relationship plates. We are to be friendly with and honor everyone, but we cannot be close, intimate friends with everyone.

So we name, prayerfully, while submitting ourselves to the imperatives of Scripture. When we name, it should not elicit in us a need to protect or maintain, to cling or clamor. Naming, rather, should elicit praise and thanksgiving to the God who has given us "our" people for such a time as this.

Name Your People Out Loud

I've found it helpful at times to also name out loud. I'm not saying I ask a friend for coffee and pester them with questions about whether we're friends or not. Please, whatever you do, don't corner another woman with the pleading, "Can we be friends?" or the pressurized, "I want to be friends with you." A good rule of thumb is that if you have to ask or demand, it's probably not a close friendship.

I have found it helpful, however, to throw around the word *friend* with those who are written in the margins of my journal, as in "I'm thankful you're my friend," or "You are a friend I can share things with," or even "You are a friend who feels like family." If they don't think of me that way, they can run far away in the opposite direction—and that definitely helps to make things clear—but if they also consider me a friend, those words go a long way in clarifying and solidifying our friendship.

Sometimes you and I are going to have moments when the emotional alarms are going off because we feel alone or hormonal or some crazy concoction of the two. Let's not panic or go into self-pity mode. Let's simply go again to the question, turn it over in prayer, and let God answer it for us: *Who are my people?*

And if you truly don't have people yet because you've just moved to town or you're in a new situation, go be the people for someone else. Keep pushing through the awkward, inviting people into your personal space, and sharing your stories. In time, you will be able to name too.

PART FOUR

Being a Friend

FIFTEEN

Back and Forth

Listen Well

Be quick to listen [and] slow to speak.

James 1:19 NIV

*M*ost conversations between friends are like a tennis match: words go back and forth and back and forth. Questions are lobbed, answered, and pitched back.

But then there are *those* people and *those* conversations. Instead of a tennis match, their conversations are more like the end of a basketball game when one team is trying to run down the clock. The point guard dribbles for a while, then starts a series of passes between the players, and no one is really doing anything except wishing away the final seconds. The other team's players, unless they choose to foul, never touch the ball. They look helplessly on, powerless to stop the passing and not feeling very much a part of the game. (Aren't you proud of me for using a sports analogy? Go me! That was for the one man who will read this book. *Hi, Kyle.*)

In other words, the conversation is one-sided.

I've been the helpless basketball team in conversations *way* too often. I know I'm in a one-sided conversation when, forty-five minutes in, after I've been listening and listening and listening, I start having a separate conversation in my head, with myself. It goes something like this:

> Demanding thought: *I kind of want to scream right now.*
>
> Rebuttal polite thought: *Keep nodding and smiling. Muster some sort of response when appropriate.*
>
> Demanding thought: *I am so stuck. How will I ever get out of this conversation? Who will come save me?*
>
> Rebuttal polite thought: *Don't get lost. Focus on the mouth. Hear the words. Process the words.*
>
> Demanding thought: *Interrupt and try to say something. Whatever you do,* do not *ask another question. I repeat,* do not *ask another question.*

Most of the time, I go ahead and ask another question, hoping, I suppose, that there is a clock somewhere silently ticking down and a buzzer will go off and magically end this thing.

The Bible tells us we should think about how we want others to treat us and then treat them that very same way. How do we want others to approach us? How do we want others to include and invite us? How do we want to be talked about when we're not in the room? How much do we want the benefit of the doubt? And how do we want others to treat us in conversation?

I want to get to know the person I'm talking to but I also want to be known by them. I want to hear not just the person's words but their emotions and heart's desires, and I also want them to hear mine. In other words, I want the tennis match instead of the lopsided basketball game.

My point is that, when it comes to friendship, we must sharpen our question-asking and listening skills. Those skills are essential to discovering and deepening friendships. So if you talk too much, you should stop that. If you talk over people, you should stop that. If you're doing most of the talking in a relationship, you should stop that. If you ask questions without actually listening for answers before you jump in with a response, you should stop that too. All of these things are genuine hindrances to your friendships, and your friends have asked me to tell you this.

Turn Outward

I'm going to put on my pastor's-wife hat for a moment and invite you to see what I see. Because of my role and because I get to spend time with women all across the country, I have the incredible opportunity to get to know a variety of women across a vast spectrum of backgrounds, church denominations, races, life stages, and ages. I absolutely love it. I love being invited into their lives and hearing their stories and learning how God is at work in and through them.

However, I also hear stories of relationship struggles and I see women struggling to connect with others, just as I do myself sometimes. The commonality, I often discover, is that so many of us know what we want—deep friendships in which we are known—but we do not think about how often our attention is on ourselves and how little we turn our attention onto others. We think that in order to be known we should just start talking. It is counterintuitive in many ways, but the truth is that in order to be known we must *stop* talking and start asking questions and actively listening. These actions are those of a biblical friend and they lay the groundwork for a warm, safe, meaningful, *mutual* friendship.

Recently I spoke at a conference, and during a Q&A time, a woman asked how she could become friends with her pastor's wife. She was frustrated that her pastor's wife seemed aloof and unapproachable. Upon further probing, I discovered that she assumed rights to this woman as a friend and was frustrated that the pastor's wife hadn't come toward her with friendship. What it boiled down to was that she simply wanted to be known by the pastor's wife and to have unobstructed access to her—which is not friendship. Friendship is mutual; it's a back-and-forth thing like the tennis match. A true friend doesn't just want to be known. A friend also wants to know.

I probably felt a little defensive as I interacted with that woman at the conference, because I know what it's like for women to want to be around me *only* because I'm the pastor's wife and they have some need to be known by their pastor's wife. I can sniff that out pretty fast, because I can feel the difference when someone is genuinely interested in me as a person. They are not concerned with themselves and who they're friends with and what kind of strange validation that can offer them; in fact, they're not concerned much with themselves at all. They show a genuine interest in me.

I think this kind of stuff happens with everyone, not just pastors' wives. But being a person who gets to see the big picture, I can tell you that a lot of our struggles come down to the way we interact with people. Are we primarily talkers or primarily listeners? That may play a bigger part in developing and deepening friendship than we have believed. When I spend time with women and they don't reciprocate my questions, I chalk it up to women needing counsel or a listening ear, which I'm happy to give, and sometimes I can tell that they feel nervous or uncertain. However, I must say that a consistent lack of question-asking over a period of time spent with someone is a dividing line for me between friendship and casual acquaintance. And I don't think I'm alone on this.

We simply cannot go wrong with asking questions and listening more, especially in this age of social media. Everywhere we turn these days we're bombarded with people sharing their every thought and displaying their lives for all to see. People are shouting to be heard, and when they don't feel heard they shout even louder. Perhaps we are so busy shouting to be heard that there is no space left to ask good questions, listen carefully, or think about what we're hearing. Perhaps the art of asking good questions is dying a painfully quick death. Or perhaps it's that we're naturally good at talking about and focusing on ourselves, and asking questions and listening require thinking beyond our own desires.

I think asking good questions and listening well are worth the effort, however, and not just because they are tools for friendship. They are key ingredients to fulfilling Jesus's command to love one another. These skills enable us to influence others and speak grace, hope, and life into the lives of others. Within the church, good questions and good listening kill the assumptions we make about others that often exacerbate divisions and gaps between us. How can we love and bear with one another if we don't know and listen to one another?

Consider Job and his friends. Job's friends showed up on his doorstep, sat with him silently for seven days (good!), and then, without asking a single question, started spouting off counsel, all of which came from their own experiences and assumptions (bad!). If they'd only asked a few questions and listened well to Job's grief, they might have truly comforted him and offered him solid hope rather than compounding his grief.

Job's friends offer us "what not to do" wisdom through their lack of questions—we see more clearly that our goal in asking questions and listening well is not to gather information as a gossip or busybody might do but rather so that we might serve our friend in some way, such as offering empathy or helpful counsel. So much can be helped and so much can be diffused by a few well-placed questions.

Tell Me More

My relationship with my friend Ishan blossomed almost as quickly as a bud opening on a time-lapse camera, all because of one simple question. It was about race. Ishan is black and I am white, and in one of our very first conversations she pointedly asked me how I felt about her and her family attending our church. I admit that I was completely taken aback. Had I conveyed that I felt anything but gladness at their presence in our church family? And so began a conversation about racial relations in our city. Her question was a permission slip for us to talk about something that is often difficult to discuss, and it was an open door for me to ask her questions about her experience as a black woman. I continue to this day to be thankful for that initial question, because I've had the opportunity to ask my own of her. She's shared things with me that have opened my eyes and given me empathy and love for people who experience this world differently than I do.

Being friends with Ishan has taught me the wisdom of the simple question, "Would you tell me more?" With anyone, this key unlocks door upon door. *Tell me more about what it's like to be a single mom. Tell me more about how you're feeling since your mom was diagnosed with cancer. Tell me more about the joys and difficulties of raising a child with special needs. Tell me more about your work that you're clearly so passionate about.* The best conversations involve "tell me more."

"Tell me more" is about seeking to understand the heart behind someone's words. We typically start conversations strictly with the facts—who, what, and where—but "tell me more" allows us a peek inside at a friend's emotions—the how and why. The how and why are what make people feel known and heard.

In having these conversations, however, we have to be willing to listen to the answers without jumping to conclusions, getting defensive, or making assumptions. Our opinions and perspectives may be poked at or altered in some way, as mine were with Ishan. We don't always need to find a story from our own experience to attempt to relate, because sometimes we actually can't relate. An attempt to pull from experience was one of Job's friends' fatal flaws.

It's necessary to note that a friend doesn't just ask questions and listen carefully; she also keeps secure what she's been entrusted with. Proverbs 17:9 says, "Whoever repeats the matter separates close friends" (NIV). Repeating, sharing, and spreading the sensitive stories of our friends not only dishonors the Lord and stirs up disunity but also can destroy what we've worked so carefully to build. The secure warmth of a friendship can turn cold and distant on a loose tongue.

In essence, every single person on this planet wants to be known and loved. When we make it a point to ask questions of others and listen carefully to their responses, we show respect and value to people precisely in the way they want to be treated. Someone who shows interest in others is in turn an interesting person; give me a question-asking person and I will show you a faithful friend.

SIXTEEN

Honey

Use Words Wisely

How good is a timely word!

Proverbs 15:23 NIV

*M*y husband enjoys a good Twinkie.

Spongy, cream-filled, individually wrapped, sometimes chocolate-covered—an endless supply of Twinkies perpetually lives on at our house, always stored on the top shelf of the pantry so the kids can't see them or, if spotted, reach them.

I refuse to join him in his Twinkie obsession. First of all, I ate Twinkies in elementary school. They are kid desserts. And also, they're too small. I don't want my dessert to be over in two bites. But mostly I refuse to eat them because of their reputed shelf life. I heard somewhere that Twinkies last forever. Glancing at the long list of unpronounceable ingredients running down the side of the Twinkie box, I'm fairly certain this is true, although I won't be around in one hundred years to prove the theory. I will, however, continue to make fun of my husband for eating them and remind him that he's ingesting something that could probably last longer than him.

Although the Christine Hoover Twinkie Theory of Eternity is just that—theory—there apparently *is* one food that never goes bad: honey. Honey! I learned this salient fact from reading a trivia poster while waiting for my Ethiopian food at a restaurant in Addis Ababa. Go figure. Evidently archaeologists, digging around in ancient Egyptian tombs, at one point found centuries-old pots of unspoiled honey. I don't know that I'd want to indulge in a pot of honey that's been patiently waiting to be rescued from the clutches of a mummy for millennia, but I guess someone actually did taste it, and they discovered honey's eternal shelf life. Honey, no matter what century you harvested it, apparently never goes bad or loses its sweet taste.

Is it any wonder, then, that Scripture uses honey as a metaphor for well-placed words? Proverbs 16:24 says, "Pleasant words are like a honeycomb, sweetness to the soul and health to the bones." This would have made complete sense to the ancients, because they used honey to bind wounds and as their only source for sweetening food. Words, then, are the sweetest essence of the sweetness of a friendship.

Fitting words, encouraging words, wise words, timely words—they have a long, if not eternal, shelf life. In friendship specifically, well-placed words can change the course of a life. They are safely tucked away by the hearer, savored, and referred to often, sweet reminders from fellow sojourners of the goodness of God and kind arrows pointing us in his direction. These are words that reach down, mending long-held wounds, bringing life into the soul and into the bones.

Words for Friends

I don't often consider the power of my words, but I do consider the power that others' words have had in my life. I remember specific phrases said to me even decades ago; in fact, I remember where I was when I heard some of them and sometimes even what I was wearing at the time. I remember facial expressions and the feeling in the room. I remember who was around to hear them and how they affected me. Some of those words were like vinegar, putting new ideas in my head about myself that immediately soured as they settled in my heart. But some of those words were just the right amount of sweetness, sending me soaring on possibilities of who God had made me to be and what he might make of me.

In my adulthood, the most impactful words spoken into my life have, by far, been from friends. While decades-old words helped me uncover myself and my gifts, words from friends in adulthood have helped me traverse dark days, picked me up off the floor when I've despaired, and sharpened me with hard truths spoken in gentle love. In adulthood, we can no longer pretend that life is easy, and it's the honey-words of friends, infused by the Holy Spirit, that somehow turn all the bitter things sweet.

Our words play such an essential role in how we are as a friend to others. Words have more of a shelf life in friendship than shared experiences, proximity, and even sometimes the friendship itself. We all remember words that have wounded and others that have healed, and we could spend hours parsing those words and evaluating how others have been a friend to us through their words.

However, the Bible is much more concerned with how we use *our* words than how others have used their words to harm or help us. We are wise, then, to consider how to be a friend who dishes out honey-words and who uses everyday conversation to bless, encourage, counsel, and dispense truth. We want to be intentional with our words in our friendships, because a person who doesn't consider these things is a person who will struggle in friendship, and we don't want to struggle unnecessarily because we're flippant with our words.

Help with Words

We badly need each other's honey-words. It seems to me that we all live with an invisible bullhorn shouting in our ears, and most of the blaring words are bullet-pointed lists of our failures, weaknesses, and perfectionistic standards telling us what we *should* be doing.

One thing I know about God: he rarely shouts. He speaks to us through his Word with urgency but he never relates to us with impatience, shame, or condemnation. So this bullhorn voice? It may be our enemy, it may be the words of others echoing in our ears, it may be our own irrational thoughts, but it's not God. The shouting often overrides the truths that God loves us, is compassionate toward us, offers us hope and help, and has seeds for us to sow in this world. The bullhorn is often quite effective, especially if we're isolated from community or if we've chosen friends who speak carelessly or foolishly. It's eye-opening, however, to recognize that our friends are desperately trying to silence the bullhorn just as we ourselves are. What an opportunity we have, with honey-words, to help them! We have the chance, as Hebrews 10:24 tells us, to "consider one another in order to stir up love and good works." In this context, consider means "to observe." We are to observe our friends. *What are her gifts? What stories has God written in her life that could become an impactful ministry to others? What lies and patterns of behavior are hindering her relationship with God? What does it seem God is trying to do in her life?* As we observe, we use our words to confirm her gifts, exhort her to ministry, encourage her growth, and excite her as to what God is doing in her life. Our honey-words have the power to stir up love and good works in the lives of our friends.

Don't we desperately need this? We don't need any more deflating and unnecessary *shoulds* from other Christian women. We don't need women to waste their words on criticizing, tearing down, or putting on us their convictions regarding open-ended issues. In other words, we don't need women who use their words to turn up the volume on the bullhorn. We need women who soothe our hearts with honey. And so let it begin with us.

Honey Dispensers

The Bible tells us that righteousness plays a big part in passing out honey-words in friendship:

> The mouth of the righteous is a well of life. . . .
> The lips of the righteous feed many. (Prov. 10:11, 21)

I'm going Tina Turner on this idea: What's righteousness got to do with it?

It helps to know who the righteous are. The righteous aren't holier-than-thou people dispensing dos and don'ts. The righteous are righteous because they've been *made* righteous by God through Christ. They are recipients of grace and they know it's an unmerited gift. They are happily aware of the riches they've been given. The righteous, in fact, have a storehouse of honey—they've tasted and seen that the Lord is good—and they routinely go to that storehouse for all the love, grace, truth, and wisdom they can devour. They're full and satisfied—fat and happy, if you will—in the Lord.

The righteous know something else too. They see that the storehouse holds enough for anyone who comes hungry. They are compelled by the abundant generosity of God to take what's in that storehouse and pass it out freely. The supply is endless; there is no need to be stingy.

And so, if we want to be honey-word dispensers, we first taste the sweetness of the Lord. Then we seek out people to offer them a taste, and those in closest proximity are our friends. Like an arrow looking for its mark, we have to be intentional with our timing and choice of words. We're going for wise, biblical, life-giving words. When we do so, we put pots of honey on our friends' shelves that are sweet to their taste, pots they can return to often for encouragement and direction and help.

We are a righteous people, made so by Jesus Christ. We are people of life! But do the words we dispense among our friends reflect this? How much time do we spend instead speaking dead words that have a short shelf life—or worse, are rotting and decaying? How often do we gossip, complain, speak harshly, offer worldly counsel, spend hours talking about irrelevant and frivolous things, or say nothing at all when we have a clear opportunity to comfort or encourage? The world uses the tongue in this way—dispensing sarcasm, expressing bitterness or anger, spewing hate, and stirring up strife—and it is death to hearers. But we are people of life! We can use our words to bring dead things to life, mirroring the resurrection of Christ and our own.

Speak Grace and Truth

Jesus is described as "full of grace and truth" (John 1:14). In order to dispense honey-words to our friends, we too must make it our goal that our words be full of grace and truth. We don't want to be like Job's friends, who rightly showed up to mourn with him after his family's death but spouted words full of harsh condemnation. We also don't want to be like the fool described in Proverbs 25:20: "Like one who takes away a garment in cold weather, and like vinegar on soda, is one who sings songs to a heavy heart." We want to get it right: grace and truth. Truth and grace. Just like our Jesus.

This requires intentionality. We must first be committed to consistently seeking and savoring the Scriptures. The Holy Spirit will implant the words we read into our souls and onto our tongues. And then we must enter into time with friends seeking to bless, encourage, speak truth as needed, and talk about things that matter. We must seek out ways when we're not with our friends to do the same: send a note or a text letting them know we're thankful for them, pointing out how we see God at work in their lives, urging them forward in faith, and letting them know they're being prayed for.

Scripture gives us a good framework for what honey-words look like. First, we see what honey-words are *not*. They are not slanderous (Prov. 10:18), angry (Prov. 15:1–2), biting (Gal. 5:15), or discordant (Prov. 6:19).

Instead, they are words of encouragement: "Therefore comfort each other and edify one another" (1 Thess. 5:11). They are words of loving admonishment when it is needed: "Let the word of Christ dwell in you richly in all wisdom, teaching and admonishing one another" (Col. 3:16). They are words of wise counsel: "The sweetness of a man's friend gives delight by hearty counsel" (Prov. 27:9). They are aptly timed words: "A man has joy by the answer of his mouth, and a word spoken in due season, how good it is!" (15:23). They are words that ask for and offer forgiveness: "Confess your trespasses to one another, and pray for one another, that you may be healed" (James 5:16).

In other words, these are not sugary words. These are substantive, hearty words that provide sustenance for the soul and delight it at the same time. Some of these are words that aren't immediately sweet— words from a friend can first feel indeed like wounds. But in the end, honey-words fill storehouses for our friends that they can call upon for life. Honey-words from the storehouses of God are the backbone of a sweet, life-giving friendship.

SEVENTEEN

What Friends Are For

Enter the Adversity of Others

Each of you should use whatever gift you have received to serve others.

1 Peter 4:10 NIV

At the end of a recent summer, my friend Claire asked me to meet her for coffee. I drove out her way, and we soon sat on the front porch of an old house that had been turned into a coffee shop, she with her tea and me with my coffee. Though we were covered by the porch roof, the humid mist found us, curling the hair I'd straightened an hour before.

Claire didn't wait long to tell me her news. She looked me straight in the eye and said, "I'm sick. My cancer has returned."

Tears immediately sprang to my eyes, clouding my ability to study her expression and find the assurance there that everything was going to be OK. I didn't know what to say, because I instinctively knew this was no minor scare. She'd had cancer before, years ago, and for it to return in the same area of her body didn't sound promising. When

I'd wiped my eyes, I still didn't see her characteristic confidence in her expression but rather uncertainty as she ticked off her possible treatment options.

I reached across the table, grabbed her hands in mine, and prayed. For wisdom, for peace, for God's intervention.

Throughout the following school year, Claire sought medical intervention and her friends and family gathered around her to seek God for healing, but she didn't get better. I watched her body shrink and her heart wrestle with fear. Finally, in May, after flying out to California for her son's college graduation with her husband and five other children, she entered the hospital there with labored breathing and remained there for over one hundred days, her body valiantly fighting the consequences of cancer. Those close to the family, including my husband, flew out to minister to them in a place far from their church and community who were so eager to provide them care but were unable to do anything beyond praying and sending words of encouragement.

At home, I prayed and waited for Claire's return, trying to imagine what cancer was doing to my dear friend. I thought back to the last time I'd seen her, and I couldn't actually remember when it had been. I couldn't remember the words we'd spoken to each other or if I'd hugged her or not. I even struggled to recall her voice under the cacophony of all the chaos cancer brings.

Finally she returned home, but it was only to enter another hospital and be hooked to more tubes and machines. I still rejoiced because it meant I got to see her again. The first time I went in to see her, I was nervous. I hadn't seen her in months, and in that time, I knew, her body had been ravaged. I wasn't sure she'd recognize me and, knowing she had a trach, I wasn't sure how we'd communicate or if we'd even be able to at all. I felt like I was in over my head but also had a committed urgency to see her.

When I entered her hospital room and spoke her name, her eyes struggled to open. The machines started beeping, telling the nurses that her heart rate was shooting up.

She knew I was there.

Even though she wandered in and out of consciousness, I spoke to her as I would a friend I hadn't caught up with in a while. Whenever she fell into sleep, as she inevitably did, I prayed. She'd awaken and hold her hand up, which I quickly learned was her signal that she wanted me to hold it, so I did. She mouthed words. I stroked her hair. I told her I was thankful to call her my friend. I thirstily studied the hand I was holding; her hands reminded me of her daughters'.

When I returned the next time, and all the times after that, by all indications she wasn't conscious of my presence. But I no longer went in nervously. I went in with joy, eager to speak to her as if she could hear every word, pray for her, and simply sit by her bedside and hold her hand as the machines beeped and pulsed.

I'd never been in that situation before. I'd never sat with a friend on her deathbed. I'd never spoken to a husband preparing to lose his wife nor children preparing to lose their mother. I'd never pleaded with God from that perspective or that position, so close to the reality of death. It was a time when life and faith came into razor-sharp focus.

She died on a Friday night, just hours after Kyle and I went to see her and say goodbye.

After she died, I wanted to go back to look at text messages she'd sent me, even some from the hospital. Only then did I remember that I'd gotten a new phone while she was in the hospital in California; only then—when I finally wanted to reread them—did I realize that all of those messages were gone forever.

But I have images in my mind that remain. Of being in her retreat-like home. Of sitting with her by the fire in her bedroom with cups of tea. Of watching her watch her girls dance in *The Nutcracker*. Of her praying for me after church as I prepared to go speak to some women about grace. Of the birthday lunch she planned for me. Of her words after my husband's fortieth birthday party: "I'll always remember how happy you and Kyle were dancing together." Of the bottle of vanilla wrapped in burlap ribbon she brought back for me from Mexico.

If I stop and listen for it, I can hear the cadence of her voice when she prayed. It was beautiful, a different cadence than when she spoke, a lilting, childlike sound that conveyed absolute assurance she was heard by her Father.

Claire's death was a domino that started many others falling, and I'm working through it all. Not without help, thank God. He's given me friends who listen, offer wise counsel, and love me when I'm not put together. What I was privileged to do for Claire, my friends are doing for me, albeit in much different circumstances.

There is a reason God gives us to one another in friendship. Friends are for joy, fun, companionship, and sharpening, yes. But according to wise King Solomon, they are primarily for companionship through adversity: "A friends loves at all times, and a brother is born for adversity" (Prov. 17:17).

Friends bring ginger ale and chicken noodle soup when your kids are puking. Friends bring you meals when you've had a baby. Friends listen on the phone from miles away as you verbally process your discouragements and your joys. Friends take you to physical therapy after you've had surgery.

Friends show up at your family member's funeral. Friends pray for your marriage and won't let you take the easy way out. Friends ask the tough questions that shine light on your situation. Friends grieve when you're grieving and rejoice when you're rejoicing.

And they do all this voluntarily, with joy.

Entering Another's Adversity Is Our Honor

Our first thought when we consider friends voluntarily entering into adversity is often, *Who will do those things for me?* Or maybe, if you're in the thick of it right now, *Who is doing these things for me?* The question Scripture leads us to, however, is the opposite: Who are *we* doing this *for?*

In Galatians 6:2, Paul says, "Bear one another's burdens, and so fulfill the law of Christ." A few phrases later, he says each one is to carry his or her own load (v. 5), so he seems to make a distinction between *burden* and *load.* Indeed, unlike a load able to be carried by an individual, a burden is a weight too heavy for one person. It requires more than one. It requires a friend.

Adversity is a litmus test of friendship because it asks for us to willingly enter someone else's pain. A friend's adversity calls for our action in this pain, whether through prayer, physical help, financial help, or—perhaps the most difficult—emotional and spiritual help. Adversity asks us to sit in the same uncertainty our friend sits in, without throwing around trite answers and fix-it-quickly solutions. A friend's adversity will often test our own faith in God, because so often we cannot fix or ease their pain and, even more often, we don't really know any of the answers and can't promise guaranteed outcomes. We're simply there, walking beside her, willing to help carry the heavy weight, not pointing to our own answers but to God himself.

In doing so, we are in the will of God. We're doing exactly what he'd have us do as a friend, because *this is what we were born for.*

We're afraid sometimes to enter into others' pain because we know it's possible we might say the wrong thing or we might not have the right answers. But mostly, I think, we're afraid of the burden. When we think of burdens, we tend to think they'll be oppressive, as if we'll be suffocated by them. There *are* often heavy and difficult things that we see our friends through, but I've learned from experience that God asks us to help carry our friends' burdens *because he wants to give us joy.*

There is no greater joy than to be in the midst of an extremely difficult situation—something you've wondered if you could handle or a person could stand up under—and see God's goodness and faithfulness so tangibly expressed. Carrying burdens with and for others is where we see the certainty of our hope. It's where we truly learn the depths of God. It's where we offer to our friends not trite answers but a true and lasting hope that anchors the soul in all things—and, in turn, we're even more anchored ourselves.

Friendship is hard to come by because a lot of people don't voluntarily choose to enter into other people's worlds or into their pain. We can be people who choose to do just that; we can be who we were born to be.

I didn't expect this summer. I haven't wanted what it's given. But if I know anything now, in this mystery called life, it's something this summer taught me—that God doesn't run away from pain and death. He ran into it and he runs into it still. He swallows up mortality with unending life.

I'm not at all happy that Claire died, but I tell you that it was my great joy to be so intimately involved in both her life and her death. It was a privilege and honor to enter into her pain and the pain of her family. Although I fumbled my way through, I felt such a sense of purpose and joy, as if I was doing something I was made to do.

God isn't afraid to enter brokenness, and we shouldn't be either, because all we're really doing is bringing him into the situation anyway. We don't have to have answers. We just have to be present and willing to listen. We can't be afraid that something is too much for him or too big for him or that the answers won't be there. Sometimes the answers really won't be there, but the presence of God is *always* there. In order to be a faithful friend in adversity, we simply imitate that ministry of presence.

EIGHTEEN

One Word

Pray for Your Friends

Pray for one another.

James 5:16

When we enter into a friend's adversity, we eventually come up against a wall.

Two of my very best friends are single with a desire to be married to godly men. These two women are not waiting to live life only after they're married; they love people and serve God well in their singleness. But sometimes they have days when hoping is hard and they need to give voice to the longing in their hearts.

So I listen.

I got married not long after college, so I really have no idea what joys and difficulties singleness affords. All I know is that when my friends share their difficulties, I really, *really* want to make it all better for them. I want to magically pull a perfectly suited, godly man out of a hat for each of them. I want to search eHarmony myself for the overlooked gem. I want to matchmake, even though my prior attempts have been more like shoving square pegs into round holes than creating love connections.

I can conjure up a whole lot of answers for a whole lot of questions I'm asked in life, but why godly women are not being snatched up *immediately* is not one I have any answers for. Although I don't consider it wrong to be single, in this case it very much feels like a wrong I want to right, because I love my friends and I want them to have the desires of their hearts.

But I can't fix it.

I can listen, and I do, but I also sense my own discomfort that listening isn't enough. I want to *do something.* Anything. I can't, however, change my friends' circumstances. I can't say magic words that will ease their struggles. And if I want to be a good friend, I also can't ignore or gloss over the things turning over in their hearts, so I enter into the difficulty with few, if any, answers or helps.

This is the discomforting wall to which I refer: entering in without being able to fix.

The wall has made an appearance in my friends' difficult marriages, infertility issues, emotional problems, doubt, and sin. It's been there in children not reaching milestones, unemployment, and big life decisions. And it's been there in prodigal children, adoption obstacles, and difficult diagnoses. I cannot tear down the walls of suffering. I can't make it all better.

In fact, there are many around me who are suffering right now, and several are so close by that I am vicariously suffering too. How painful it is to see sin bear its fruit, how disheartening to encounter the stark reality of brokenness, how difficult to watch others suffer!

As a friend to the sufferers, when I come up against this wall I also recognize a tug of temptation, and this is where I must be careful.

This is where we *all* must be careful.

We Can't Fix It, but We Can Pray

As friends, we have influence, a voice, and an invitation into the path-altering moments and the daily routines of others' lives. These opportunities, I find, ask me the basic questions of who I am as a friend and what I am to do to minister to my friends.

John the Baptist exemplifies the undercurrent of temptation that the wall brings us. He appeared on the scene after four hundred years of God's silence. Naturally, those waiting for and seeking God's voice perked up at John's cry for repentance to make straight the way of the Lord. "Who are you?" they said, seeming to marvel at this one speaking so authoritatively in the echo of the prophet Elijah.

In the hanging question, temptation lurks. John the Baptist had a following. He had a ministry and a reputation that elicited crowds. He had disciples. He could've answered the question in a way that gave him a greater influence, albeit a false one. He could've answered with a guarantee to tear down some insurmountable walls. His response to the question, however, sent temptation fleeing. "He confessed, and did not deny, but confessed, 'I am not the Christ'" (John 1:20).

The temptation for John the Baptist is the temptation we face: to think of ourselves as the Christ for other people. We know we are not the actual Christ, but we're tempted to believe and act from the idea that we're able to be all-knowing, all-present, all-powerful, self-sufficient, without limits, self-existent, and in control of all things. Especially in how we minister to our friends. The very real truth is that we are not able to ease the suffering of our friends, we are entirely unable to produce spiritual change in them, and we cannot be the Spirit of God to them. There are things we can't fix. *We are not the Christ.*

This is the wall to which I refer, this wall that reminds me I can't change hearts. I can't change my heart. I know because I've tried—with behavior modification and strong will and self-made rules. I can't change my husband's heart. Believe me, I've tried, along with trying to change the hearts of my kids and every other person with whom I've come in contact.

I recognize now that it's a very good thing I can't change a heart, because I would change hearts into my image and according to my standards and in lockstep with my self-focused desires. I would rescue my friends early and often, in times when God often chooses with his greater wisdom not to rescue. I would comfort with false hopes. And I would only feed my gluttonous pride more, thinking my words were magical and my responses the needed elixir.

So when it comes to being a friend to others, I have to resist the belief that I am sovereign enough to change their circumstances, rescue them from all pain, and say or do just the right thing that will help them at the heart level.

Only God can do that.

God stands in between us and our friends, and that's exactly where we want him. That's exactly where we need him. At some level, our friends will face adversity we cannot fix or change. Any attempts to do so would only compound their issues, because we aren't and can't be their Christ. Sometimes God is wanting to do something in our friend's life—we can see it clearly and we want it for them so badly— but it requires us to let things happen without attempting to rescue them with worldly counsel or numbing concoctions or borrowed excuses.

I see this with my single friends. I want so badly to give them what they want, but I see that God has and is working specifically in their singleness, and I see that God's been faithful to them and will continue to be faithful to them, no matter if he's doing things differently than how I'd do them. I want my friends to be happy and free from struggle, but God wants their hearts and he often gets hearts through the working out and the wrestling.

If we see the wall as a frustration, we will either run from the pain of others or bulldoze them down with our own prescriptions. We won't enter into their suffering in the way that's needed, because we hate the feeling of not being able to fix things and we don't want the responsibility of bearing an ongoing burden we can't solve.

The wall is a good thing, however, because it reminds us that there is something we *can* do.

———

Doesn't God stand between us and our friends? Doesn't he have access to their hearts and to ours? Can't he do a work of change or sanctification in the unseen places? And hasn't God given us a way to plead for the movement of his hands?

We can pray! We can talk to him about their pain. We can intercede for him to intercede. We can ask the One who can change the heart or the circumstance to actually change the heart or the circumstance. In other words, we can be like the men who carried their paralytic friend to Jesus in order that Jesus might heal him. Jesus, who responded by directing his healing first toward the man's heart and then toward his circumstances, can do the same for our friends. We have direct access to the Heart-Changer when we carry our friends to him through prayer.

Last December, when it seemed everyone online was choosing "one word" to describe their focus or goals for the new year, the Lord instead challenged me to consider "one word" for each of my closest friends and consistently pray those words over them throughout the year. Knowing their life circumstances and how God had been working in their lives, I prayerfully considered each friend and instantly had my words:

healing

miracle

grace

gift

dependence

wisdom

comfort

I wrote my words on a sticky note that has traveled with me in my Bible as I've read it this year. I've prayed for my friends, sometimes literally just one word, other times more extensive pleas focused on that one word. And can I tell you? I've seen God answer these prayers in tangible and profound ways. The miracle is currently underway. The healing came and that friend is now offering it to someone else in her same situation. One friend is learning dependence. The one needing comfort continues to receive it from the Lord.

The gift? I've prayed that word for one of my single friends, and the Lord has seen fit to not answer.

Yet.

In facing that wall, however, I refuse to try to blow through it with my own plans or to walk away dejected. I will not give up. I don't have answers and I can't change her circumstances, but I can listen *and I can pray.*

I'm not my friend's Christ, but I know Who is.

NINETEEN

Room to Breathe

Temper Expectations

[Bear] with one another.

Ephesians 4:2

I recognize in myself a deep desire to be known and understood. From Facebook and Twitter, I gather that we all have this desire in common; there is an almost desperate and sometimes angry clamor for others to understand the challenges associated with everything from certain occupations to marital statuses to childrearing to age to generational characteristics. All these words ("Open Letters," anyone?) may have only served to make us afraid—afraid to say the wrong thing, afraid to empathize or relate, afraid to dare enter into the lives of others. Ironically, as our desire to be known turns even the slightest bit sour, we are more at a distance from others than ever before.

I myself have been a desperate and angry clamorer, even in my friendships. I have at times *craved* for those around me to walk in my shoes, and this craving, I admit, has led to self-righteousness and pity for myself and subsequent pain for others. Even when some have tried to walk in my shoes, internally I've pounced on their efforts: *You don't get it.*

Recently, I experienced a time of pressing from the Lord. Without advanced warning, God called me to answer for myself, pointing to something about myself I hadn't yet seen. Isn't it amazing that we can be so completely blind to our own sin? And then one day God takes our hand and graciously and patiently points it out, and only then is it so clear.

In those moments, I am prone to despair. I'm embarrassed and overwhelmed. I want to look away and perhaps pretend I never saw it in the first place. True to form, I want to look away now.

I haven't slept well. I wake in the night and my mind takes me places I don't want to go. I can feel the spiritual pull battling over my soul, one toward despair in the here and now and the other toward hope somewhere to come. I fear falling into the abyss if I let the pressing continue, but I also fear desiring to quiet the clamor more than I desire true repentance and cleansing. It's difficult to look at sin and at the same time look at God and trust that he hasn't grown weary of me. It's not natural to run to a holy God for help when all your unholiness is showing.

There is a place, however, that I want to go with my pain: I want to go to my friends. I want to talk, laying out all my disconnected thoughts so that my friends can connect them for me. I want to look to them for comfort, assurance, and love. I want to look to them for answers.

But the problem is that this is the very sin for which God is calling me into account. He's showing me how much I look to others for approval, admiration, and validation instead of coming to him. He's pointing out how this craving has actually been self-destructive and detrimental to the very friendships I want to turn toward, because it's putting too much weight on the wrong shoulders. He's asking me to acknowledge the building resentment and frustration in my heart and, when it occurs in the future, to see those feelings as a red flag.

These kinds of cravings, whether voiced or kept hidden, breed conflict among friends. Of course, there are countless seeds for conflict in friendship—harsh words, neglect, misunderstandings, differing priority levels given to the friendship, a lack of sensitivity, or even differing personalities—but at the very heart of ongoing conflict often lies an unmet craving. Perhaps it's for validation, to feel chosen, to be liked above another, to be fully supported always, to have that one perfect friend who never disappoints, or to have constant companionship. When those cravings aren't met, the Bible says our internal desires for self-focused pleasure go to war within us, and that war's fruit—jealousy, envy, gossip, self-loathing, distancing, comparison, self-pity—spills out and over into our relationships. We become walking wounds, looking for our salve in others, and each time we're inevitably disappointed by another, our wounds split open all over again and we bristle. Sometimes we strike out in loud, dramatic ways, and other times we seethe in quiet, hidden ways, all with the same words pounding in our hearts: *It's not enough.*

Do you know why it's not enough? Do you know why this desire turns to craving and gives birth to resentment? Do you know why we're so easily hurt and offended, even when others try to enter into our lives and actually befriend us?

Because we've taken a good desire to be known and understood and laid it, seeking, at the feet of people. We've crafted people into our gods, requesting a satisfying drink of love out of broken cisterns. We've believed that if people just *finally* understood or *finally* became the friends we're looking for, somehow the challenges we face would be eased or erased altogether. Somehow we'd find peace in the midst of our difficulty. Somehow we'd feel better. Somehow we'd be satisfied.

Sometimes a friend is who we seek them to be, and a sense of satisfaction settles in for a time. We think we've found the elusive elixir we've sought, although it vanishes through the cracks in the cistern as quickly as it came.

Do you know why? Because only God can give the validation and love we long for. Only God can meet our needs perfectly. Only God can know us fully. Proverbs 14:10 says, "The heart knows its own bitterness, and a stranger does not share its joy." In other words, no one can fully know our joy or our grief. We can spend fifty years enjoying an intimate group of besties and they will never know us anywhere close to how God knows us already at this very moment. *Other people don't have the capacity God does, so we shouldn't expect God-like capacity from them.*

The good news is that we have the Christ. Through him, we have access to the ear of our Father God, who actually requests that we throw all of our needs and cares upon his strength. He is a cistern that doesn't break. He can handle our deepest pain without running away or offending. And in trusting him, we can become perfectly OK with being a little misunderstood by others. Because we're safe, being watched over and nurtured in the most intimate parts of ourselves.

Bearing with Friends

Perhaps you've noticed that I've flipped the last chapter on its head. On one side of the coin, we see that we cannot be Christ for our friends and so we look through prayer for Christ to meet their needs. On this side of the coin, the one we're looking at now, we see that we cannot expect our friends to be Christ for us. Bonhoeffer says it like this:

> Jesus Christ stands between the lover and the others he loves. . . . As only Christ can speak to me in such a way that I may be saved, so others, too, can be saved only by Christ himself. This means that I must release the person from every attempt of mine to regulate, coerce, and dominate him with my love. The other person needs to retain his independence of me; to be loved for what he is, as one for whom Christ became man, died, and rose again, for whom Christ bought forgiveness of sins and eternal life. Because Christ has long since acted decisively for my brother, before I could begin to act, I must leave him his freedom to be Christ's; I must meet him only as the person he already is in Christ's eyes.[1]

Jesus stands between us and our friends. This is a safety valve for all of our hearts. If we turn that valve off, we suffocate our friends and weigh them down with our expectations, because what we crave can only be met in Christ. With the valve off, we turn our worship and service to the creature rather than the Creator, which Romans 1 warns is a dangerous and slippery slope toward physical, emotional, and spiritual death. Our expectations that other women can be Christ for us are sin, and these unfettered expectations will always lead to dysfunctional friendships that are rife with conflict.

So what do we do? How are we to be a friend to others in a God-honoring way that does not usurp his rightful place in their lives and in ours? We give our friends room to breathe, or as Ephesians 4:2 says, we must be patient and "[bear] with one another in love."

Bearing with one another means we don't expect perfection from our friends in how they relate to us, how they comfort us when we're hurting, how they speak to us, or how they prioritize our friendship. We think the best of our friends and cut them slack when they don't respond to us perfectly in every situation.

Bearing with one another means we overlook small offenses instead of storing up bitterness. It means we gently and lovingly address the larger offenses in a timely manner, seeking to restore the relationship. We're quick to forgive and slow to get angry, just as God is with us. We're quick to listen to how we've hurt others and just as quick to apologize. Our friends are safe with us because we're loyal and willing to see it through, even and especially when conflict arises. We persevere in our relationships.

Bearing with one another means we celebrate our friends rather than envying them. It means we let our friends be who they are, not attempting to mold them into who we *wish* they were. It means we refuse to engage in drama, manipulative charm, or control to get our friends to meet a need we have. Instead, we receive their friendship as an unwarranted gift from God. We appreciate our friends and are thankful toward God.

Bearing with one another means we don't demand that our friendships stay static. We allow our friends to grow and change as individuals, and for the friendship to evolve over time.

It means we don't fuel our selfish desires for friendships and then stomp our feet in protest when God doesn't give us what we want in the way we want it. It means we enjoy friendships, both old and new, with various people. We don't expect one person to be our catchall friend.

Bearing with one another means we help to build friendships that consistently encourage our friends to move toward Christ and toward dependence on him. It also means we choose friends who do the same for us.

In other words, bearing with one another means we're deeply committed to our friends but even more deeply committed to our Christ.

When We Need to Take a Step Back

Our commitment to keeping Christ at the center of our relationships will at times require us to step back from a friendship for our good or for the good of the other person, to give God room to breathe truth and life where it's needed.

John the Baptist, as we learned, fled from the internal temptation to exalt himself, but he was then faced with the *external* temptation of others wanting to exalt him to a Christlike position. John's disciples, the Bible says, were alarmed that so many who had been following him chose instead to follow Jesus. In their eyes it appeared as if John was losing his followers and his earthly stature, and because they admired him, they wanted to help him maintain his ministry. They wanted to exalt him; they wanted to put expectations of Christlikeness on him. John's response?

A man can receive nothing unless it has been given to him from heaven. You yourselves bear me witness, that I said, "I am not the Christ," but, "I have been sent before Him." He who has the bride is the bridegroom; but the friend of the bridegroom, who stands and hears him, rejoices greatly because of the bridegroom's voice. Therefore this joy of mine is fulfilled. He must increase, but I must decrease. (John 3:27–30)

John the Baptist would not let others attribute qualities to him that solely belonged to Christ. He said, "I am not the Christ. I bear witness of the Christ. I rejoice in the Christ. I point to the Christ. I exalt the Christ, not myself."

Sometimes women want or expect others to be their savior. They don't use that specific language, but they look to others for help, guidance, and love that only Christ himself can give. When we are on the receiving end of savior expectations, like John the Baptist was, we must point our friends to the real Christ and not exalt our own wisdom, abilities, or counsel: "I am not the Christ. I bear witness to the Christ and his wisdom, abilities, and counsel." In other words, we walk alongside them as fellow sojourners and willing vessels who are also in desperate need of the Christ.

If a friend is resistant to keeping Christ as the Christ in our friendship, we love them best by refusing to be their idol. We should honor them with our words and actions but we must not entangle ourselves in a destructive, idolatrous, and worldly relationship. We must simply keep pointing them to Christ and urging them to his side for the wisdom, love, and provision they seek.

When we give our friends room to breathe, it keeps God at the center of our friendships and it also gives God room to work. By refusing to be a savior to our friends, by resisting the temptation to swoop in and rescue, we are declining to elbow our way into the space where only God can move. Our friends need to meet God in that space more than they need anything from us. Are we an aspect of God's provision in each other's needs? Absolutely! But God is a jealous enough God that he will not allow one single person to take his spot as our constant need-meeter. And he has not called us to be the constant need-meeter for one single person.

So we share with others what we're feeling and how we're struggling through life, yes, and we walk with friends in their needs, but not with the expectation that we are a savior for one another. Our greatest efforts, instead, go into *seeking to understand others*—entering into the grief and joy of others as much as we humanly can, offering compassion and truth and mercy. This is biblical friendship, this is the church—esteeming others above ourselves and bringing one another, over and over, into the love and care of our Father, not seeking a savior in anything but the Savior.

TWENTY

Faithful Wounds

Speak the Truth in Love

Open rebuke is better than love carefully concealed.

Proverbs 27:5

*I*t was a crisp, blue-sky day, but I walked toward our chosen meeting spot with a sense of foreboding.

Deep in thought, unaware of people and cars passing me by, I rehearsed what I would say, searching for the words that best conveyed my intentions but knowing all along that no matter which words I chose, they would likely hurt and, even more, would likely be misunderstood. I would say them nonetheless, because I loved her and I wanted the very best for her, and I couldn't bear to see her self-destruct.

Not another one.

I'd been down this road before, just a few years prior, with another close friend, and I'd seen the wreck of lives smashing together with the force of betrayal, anger, and pride. I'd gone to her too, more than once, pleading, trying desperately to understand and to be patient and to forgive and to say all the right things. I believed then that my words, if I chose them carefully, could magically alter the situation, could bring a sister back from the edge. I believed in her too, that she would in the end do the right thing, and I vowed to be there to receive her at her return.

My pleading words did nothing. Though I said them with all the best intentions, they were imperfect and at times unnecessarily painful, and they were ultimately twisted and manipulated and misunderstood. She didn't want to hear.

I was scared for her but I also feared I'd ruined it all. My words had such little impact, after all.

And here I was again. Same song, different verse, yet I was perhaps even more afraid the second time. I knew what could happen. These were weighty matters—the course of lives could be altered—and I had to face all the possible outcomes of being a friend who confronts.

My words could dissipate, unheard, into the air.

My words could be twisted.

My intentions could be questioned.

My life also could be found lacking when combed through for sin. Who was I, after all?

My words might be unnecessarily harsh or careless or misplaced.

My relationship with her might not be close enough; perhaps others could have a more influential reach.

And, perhaps what I feared most, our friendship could break apart.

Or, *or*—please, God, let it be—she could turn away from sin and into the loving embrace of Jesus, the whole reason I was willing to do what I so dreaded.

Love Addresses

The Bible says a friend is someone who confronts sin and rebukes those they love. In my life and friendships, I have had a difficult time reconciling loving someone with judging and rebuking them. I know that confronting sin is the right thing to do, in theory, but in practice it is often messy, uncomfortable, and feels like the exact wrong thing to do. I'd much rather offer encouragement and cheerleading to a friend than possibly jeopardize our friendship by addressing her sin. But through the discomfort of "going there" with friends, I've learned that just because something is uncomfortable doesn't mean it's wrong. It just means confronting a friend is a serious matter and we need to be very, very careful in how we do it. Letting a person do whatever they want is not love, despite how the world tries to define it. Love is not passive, and it will not knowingly allow a friend to self-destruct. To truly love someone is to want the very best for them, and the very best for them is their unhindered relationship with God. If sin mutes that relationship, and it does, then we love our friends best by helping them see what is hampering their joyful and right living.

This is how God relates to us. He confronts us and convicts us of sin, all with the goal of bringing us into right relationship with him so we can enjoy a full and abundant life. He loves us enough to discipline us, just as a good father chastens his child. We are called to mirror that type of love with our friends, warning them away from sin and inviting them to return to God.

To be honest, my discomfort has shown me that my desire to avoid confronting sin in others is because I love myself and my own comfort more than I love my friends and their joy.

Again, none of this feels good, but that's OK, because we *should* feel uncomfortable. If we enjoy confrontation we're probably doing it wrong. When Paul confronts sin in the Corinthian church, his words drip with distress: "For out of much affliction and anguish of heart I wrote to you, with many tears, not that you should be grieved, but that you might know the love which I have so abundantly for you" (2 Cor. 2:4). Biblical confrontation is rooted in a deep love for our friends. Proverbs characterizes it, in fact, as a faithful wound: "Faithful are the wounds of a friend" (27:6). Tim Keller describes a faithful wound as a purposeful and exact cut: "Like a surgeon, true friends cut you in order to heal you."[1]

Faithful. *Because it reflects the Lord's love toward us.*
Purposeful. *Because there is a goal in all faithful wounds.*

Exact. *Because it is specific, methodical, and careful.*

Wounding. *Because it will hurt for a time.*

Careful Steps

I've always been terrified by the tightrope walkers at the circus. My stomach is in knots the whole time they're crossing that little rope hundreds of feet in the air while juggling or riding a bike or jumping around. I am absolutely convinced they're going to make a mistake, so I much prefer to watch what is happening on the ground, where no one can fall and break their necks in front of a live audience. As they're performing, I stare down, listening to the oohs and aahs of the crowd to ascertain how it's going, and I think about the very first time the tightrope walker went across that rope. There was a first time—there always is a first time—and I'm sure they were as terrified as I am for them in this moment.

I am not a tightrope walker, and I can guarantee I never will be, but I envision tightrope walking is similar to faithfully wounding a friend. Tightrope walkers, I would imagine, have a well of wisdom they pass down to each other—they learn a method and are careful to precisely practice that method. We, too, have clear instruction on the why and how of confronting our friends, and we must take the same care in each step as a tightrope walker does going across the circus arena so many feet in the air.

Here are our careful, methodical steps.

1. *If you are concerned for a friend, you need to pray about why.* I find that usually my feeling of concern means I am simply to pray for that friend, or I am to consider if the unsettledness is about me and the way I'm doing something in the friendship. Sometimes it means I am to pray further about bringing something to my friend's attention or asking a carefully placed question.

2. *Think and pray more.* Do not rashly broach a difficult subject with a friend. Ask God for confirmation about what he's saying to you. Ask

him to check your motives in possibly bringing this up and to give you his perspective on the situation. Is he asking you to confront? Do you need to give it more time? What exactly needs to be confronted, and how will you do so?

3. *Love.* Galatians 6:1 says that we are to restore our friends with an underlying spirit of gentleness. Are you able to approach your friend in love or are you more interested in being right or in getting your friend to do what *you* want them to do? Are you angry? Do you want their best or do you want your best? Are you close enough to your friend that you've established an emotionally connected relationship? Ask God to fill you with love and compassion for your friend.

4. *Place the goal before you.* Galatians 6:1 also says that the goal of any confrontation is restoration. If this isn't your goal, what is? Are you willing to see this through until restoration happens, even if it is years down the road? Are you willing to exhibit patience toward your friend in the process of their change or restoration?

5. *Be discreet.* Do not talk about the situation with anyone other than your friend. Sometimes I confirm with my husband what God is leading me to do, because I know he will counsel me wisely. But I've found that my tendency is to want to seek out multiple people and discuss what I'm seeing with them, as if talking about it with them will make the situation go away or cause God to release me from the responsibility of addressing the issue. This desire to talk about it with others is poorly motivated and, if I act on it, I actually become an *unfaithful* wounder. Biblical confrontation between friends is just that: between friends, unless and until others need to be brought in.

6. *Be a truth-teller.* At some point, after much prayer and consideration, the truth needs to be told. We must be gentle in our demeanor and word choice, but faithful friends don't skirt the truth. Honestly, most of the faithful wounds I inflict are not dramatic. They happen in everyday situations when I point a friend in a specific direction as they're making decisions or wrestling with an issue, or when I offer them counsel. Sometimes the truth is hard to hear and even harder to say, but it's my responsibility as a faithful friend. Am I pointing them toward true

hope in Christ and toward biblical imperatives or am I feeding them false hopes? In some cases, especially if we're offering truth our friends may not want, the words are going to be painful for our friends to hear and they're going to be painful for us to say, but we honor the Lord by loving our friends in this way. We must love them enough that we're willing to initiate our own pain for the benefit of others.

7. *Be willing to confess your own sins.* Proverbs 27:9 says, "The sweetness of a friend comes from his earnest counsel" (ESV). *Earnest* means "from the heart," and *counsel* means "to tell someone a secret." In other words, we are to be self-revealing, and we're to offer truth and counsel that are reassuring ("[this] is common to man" [1 Cor. 10:13]) but also sharpening.

8. *Be ready with wise counsel.* If your friend is willing to hear you, praise God! Be ready to encourage your friend down the path toward restoration, which God has readily made for them and clearly laid out in Scripture: confess and repent and be reconciled to God and restored to others.

9. *Be ready to forgive.* After Paul confronted a man who was affronting God with his blatant sin, the man repented. Paul offers counsel on how friends can respond to the repentant: "You ought rather to forgive and comfort him, lest perhaps such a one be swallowed up with too much sorrow. Therefore I urge you to reaffirm your love to him" (2 Cor. 2:7–8).

With faithful wounds, we walk on a tightrope carefully, relying fully on the Holy Spirit. In everything—every methodical step—we love.

On that bright, blue-sky day, I did indeed muster up the courage to talk about what I had been seeing in my friend's life. She listened, but I could tell my words weren't hitting the target I intended. I told her I loved her and that I was trying to show it, but I left that lunch feeling awful.

My words had dissipated into the air, just as I'd feared. Maybe I could have tweaked them a little or handled them differently. Believe me, I've gone back over them with a fine-tooth comb and seen clearly all the fumbles and missteps.

But I don't regret doing it. I'm glad I said something, because if there's one thing I've learned about being a truth-teller, it's that conviction and change aren't up to me. God's got that covered. I'm simply to love, to mirror how he loves me.

I pray for their restoration, and I pray that one day my friends will see that the wounds I inflicted upon them were the wounds of a friend.

TWENTY-ONE

Homesick

Display Joy in Jesus

Keep your conduct among the Gentiles honorable, so that when they speak against you as evildoers, they may see your good deeds and glorify God.

1 Peter 2:12 ESV

I am, to put it mildly, an enthusiastic, self-appointed ambassador of Texas. Because I don't currently live in Texas and haven't for over eight years now, I've kept my Texas spirit alive by taking it upon myself to represent my home state to my fellow Virginians. Whenever someone is willing to allow all my obnoxiousness to show, I will thoroughly exhaust my persuasive arguments as to why Texas is what I refer to as "the Great State."

In order to persuade you, dear reader, about the Great State, I call Exhibit #1: pictures of my toddler-aged boys sitting among mounds of bluebonnets, wearing cute Aggie overalls. *Please ignore that they're sitting one hundred feet from a highway with cars going by at eighty-five miles per hour.*

Exhibit #2: Friday night lights, the actual ones. The sixteen-year-old quarterback as hero, bearing the weight of an entire community. The pep rallies and multimillion-dollar high school stadiums. The whole town at the game. *Please ignore the fact that high school and college football are considered by some to be a religion.*

Exhibit #3: *Friday Night Lights*, the television show. *Clear eyes, full heart, can't lose!* There is absolutely nothing negative to write about this television show. Texas forever!

Exhibit #4: Beef as BBQ. Do not come at me with your pork or North Carolina vinegar-based sauce rebuttals.

I conclude my persuasive argument with the clincher, Exhibit #5: Tex-Mex. Please pass the queso! And the chips and salsa, the enchiladas smothered in cheese, and the sopapillas! *Please ignore the calories.*

My friend Amy went to Texas for the first time this year, and seeing as how I couldn't go with her, and being the great ambassador that I am, I exhaustively prepared her for it and made her promise to live-text me throughout her entire trip. As soon as she got off the plane in Dallas and started driving through the state, I asked for three words to describe her first reactions. I was fully expecting "great" and "state" to pop up on my phone, but instead she chose "wide-open" and "pawnshops." *Pawnshops?* Did she not see the kindly old men wearing their cowboy hats? Did she not enjoy the friendly hospitality from the moment she stepped off the plane? Did she not start swooning at her first "y'all" and "fixin' to"? Did she not taste the breakfast tacos? *Hello?*

In my now-home of Virginia, as soon as I pull out my clincher Exhibit #5, Tex-Mex, I'm met with nods and helpful looks, so I naively think I'm getting somewhere (and that I'm an excellent persuasive speaker).

"Oh, so you've had Tex-Mex?" I ask, thinking I've finally found a kindred spirit.

"Oh, yes, have you been to _____?" (Insert one of a handful of authentic Mexican food places in our city.)

I sigh, pat them on the head while holding back the words "Bless your heart," and, as the good ambassador that I am, patiently explain to my uncultured friend the *vast* difference between Tex-Mex and

Mexican food. When we first moved to Virginia, I couldn't put words to the difference, but the more I tried the Mexican food places in our city, the more I discovered the primary differences: Texans eat tacos for breakfast and they smother everything in cheese, lots and lots of cheese. *Please ignore where the Lone Star State falls in the rankings of most obese states.*

If my dear Virginian friends failed to grasp the richness of Tex-Mex from my persuasive arguments alone, I've found a better way to get my point across: invite them over for dinner and serve Tex-Mex—homemade salsa, homemade guacamole, refried beans, rice, fajitas, individually fried hard taco shells, and enchiladas. Tasting and experiencing trumps talking any day.

As much as I try to persuade people about Texas, however, Virginia and all its people have done a little persuading on me, just by being downright wonderful. I love it here. In fact, it's become so much of a home that now I feel as if I have a home in two places.

I've learned that these longings for a true home are simply whispers of something to come. As C. S. Lewis says in *The Weight of Glory*:

> These things—the beauty, the memory of our own past—are good images of what we really desire; but if they are mistaken for the thing itself, they turn into dumb idols, breaking the hearts of their worshippers. For they are not the thing itself; they are only the scent of a flower we have not found, the echo of a tune we have not heard, news from a country we have never yet visited.[1]

"Friday Night Lights" and "Virginia Is for Lovers" aside, the home that my soul truly longs for is my home in heaven with God. That home is my truest home, the place I will one day live the longest and enjoy the most. The thing is I may be a self-appointed ambassador of Texas, but God has *actually* appointed me as an ambassador of that true home.

And the primary avenue I have for representing him to people who don't know him, people who don't know anything about my true home, is through friendship. Oswald Chambers expresses our goal and hope in pursuing friendships with nonbelievers: "You can never give another person that which you have found, but you can make him homesick for what you have."[2]

The Heart Speaks Louder than Behaviors

After begging and begging us, my middle son was granted permission to start playing soccer this year. We've now entered the team sports world, which means juggling games on both Saturdays and Sundays. And there's the rub: Sunday games for a pastor's household can be the difference between playing and not playing a sport. So I signed him up with trepidation, anxious to see the final practice and game schedule.

In the meantime, I had a conversation with a friend whose child also signed up, a friend who is not a Christian. We talked about what time the Sunday games might be, and, to this woman who knows we are Christians, who knows my husband is a pastor, who has discussed matters of faith with me, who has been invited to our church multiple times, I complained about the difficulty of juggling church and outside activities. *I complained.*

I didn't realize what I'd done until later. I thought back on the conversation and realized that I'd made it sound like church and my husband's job are burdens for us and that, without either, life would be so much easier. What was I communicating to her about being a follower of Christ? I was communicating that it's intertwined with annoying and burdensome requirements. And who wants that?

As an ambassador, I wasn't painting an accurate picture of my God, and I certainly wasn't painting a *beautiful* picture that might stir up homesick longings in her heart.

That conversation and subsequent conviction got me thinking about whether my life and conversation and attitude differ from those of my unbelieving friends. *Do they? And how should they differ?*

When I think of how my life should differ from those of my unbelieving friends, I tend to think in terms of behaviors: the way I do or don't watch certain things, the way I relate to money or food or drink, the way I serve, the way I dress, or how much I read my Bible or pray or attend church gatherings. The friend I had that conversation with, however, is like me in many of these ways: she serves people, she is a great mom and friend, and she loves her husband well. Perhaps the only behavioral difference is that she doesn't go to church or read the Bible.

I think most of us think of being set apart from the world in terms of behavior. We value holy living, which is not a bad thing at all and is in fact an important aspect of reflecting our holy God to a world that doesn't know him. But as I began to think about what difference my friend might see in me that would cause her to consider the beauty of Christ and desire him herself, I realized that it would be more of the heart attitudes displayed through word and deed: joy, peace, hope, dependence, sacrificial love, forgiveness and reconciliation, long-suffering, generosity, thankfulness, faithfulness, and all the other words that appear in the "put on" passages in Scripture. According to Paul, those are the captivatingly stunning qualities that make us shine as lights in the world.

> Do all things without complaining and disputing, that you may become blameless and harmless, children of God without fault in the midst of a crooked and perverse generation, among whom you shine as lights in the world, holding fast the word of life. (Phil. 2:14–16)

Too often we differ from the world in behavior but not in our heart attitudes. We are fearful, we worry, we are proudly self-sufficient, we hold grudges, we don't always keep our word, and we complain out of ungratefulness. What is this communicating to our unbelieving friends about our God?

I had to ask this of myself, because do I not have hope? Do I not have within me the Spirit who is the source of all joy and peace and love? Do I not have everything I need for life and godliness? These treasures are what I want to communicate to my unbelieving friends about the goodness of our God and what he's done for all those who believe. These treasures stir up longing that can only be described as homesickness.

So let us be friends who are also ambassadors. Let us not just talk about how we know and love God; let's show the beauty of Spirit-grown righteousness so well that our friends can practically *taste* it. People will be curious about our home country. They may want to visit and possibly even uproot it all and plant themselves at the feet of Jesus.

Make them homesick for what you have.

And, friends, if you go to Texas? Please ignore all the concrete, the insane number of billboards, the all-fried buffets, and the season the Cowboys just had.

Oh, and the pawnshops.

TWENTY-TWO

Hashtag Friendship

Enhance Offline Relationships Online

Whatever you do, do it all for the glory of God.
1 Corinthians 10:31 NIV

*E*very day, all day, we each hold a minuscule thing in our hands that can be either a weapon of destruction for ourselves and others or a helpful tool for connecting us with our friends.

I'm speaking, of course, about our phones.

With our various schedules and responsibilities, it's much more rare that we get to sit across from a friend face-to-face than it is we're able to shoot texts back and forth throughout the day or comment on a friend's status update or Instagram picture. Social media and quick connections through texting have added an element of ease to our relationships, but they have also added a layer of complication that is often difficult to navigate.

"Hashtag friendship," or friendship that happens through our phones, isn't always true friendship. Sometimes, in scrolling through Facebook, I glance at a status update and cannot for the life of me remember who this "friend" is or how I know them. I comment on the Instagram pictures of people I've never met in real life and likely never will and, in doing so, somehow feel like I have a relationship with them.

We all kind of know that hashtag friendship isn't necessarily true friendship, and it's therefore fashionable to denigrate social media with our mouths while scrolling and swiping and typing away with our hands. We know our phones aren't always good for us or our real-life friendships but we fear missing out or not knowing what's going on, so we stay on social media while harboring a love/hate relationship with it.

I'm not knocking social media or cell phone use. There is, of course, absolutely so much that can go wrong with social media. But there is so much that can go right too. In fact, social media is not a negative or a positive; it is a neutral communication medium that reveals, quite well actually, a person's priorities, motivations, passions, and beliefs. You can learn a lot about someone based upon their Twitter or Instagram feed.

But it reveals something else too: the hearts of those who consume it. Everyone knows that sinking feeling of finding something on social media that hits a sensitive spot—some that we're very aware of and some that we didn't realize were sensitive until we saw *that* post.

In fact, let's go straight to the source right now. Pop with me over to Facebook or, if you're not on Facebook, to the text messages on your phone. You know, for official research. Scroll down for a bit and note what feelings arise.

The Conversation We're Having

Oh, heavens, so sorry to leave you there for that long while I scrolled through the important updates in the lives of my hundreds of closest friends. Time got away from me. But what a hilarious video of cats jumping away from cucumbers! And did you see that Jimmy Fallon lip sync battle! And how cute are your kids!

What did your research show? My research showed that my Facebook friends:

Receive funny texts from their teenage children, as evidenced by screen shots.

Appear to have spent hours decorating their mantels.

Try to be casual about the fact that they want you to buy something from them.

Encounter many must-read, life-changing articles, indicated by headlining the shared article with one word: THIS.

Are extremely frustrated/happy about the current state of world affairs.

Are #blessed.

Feelings I felt: annoyance, happiness, ambivalence, and thankfulness. Quite the mix.

But you don't need my official research, because your feed and your feelings—if you haven't given up on social media entirely—are probably exactly the same.

I asked women on social media—where else?—how it causes them angst in friendship, and they mentioned things like jealousy and bitterness and comparison and a fear of missing out. I also noticed an interesting theme, however, and it's something I very much see in myself as well: when it comes to hashtag friendship, we tend to view ourselves as passive recipients or even victims of drive-by hashtags. When it comes to the way people use social media, we are quick to point out the speck in someone else's eye but fail to acknowledge the (b)log in our own. (Sorry, couldn't resist.)

In other words, our litany of complaints about social media tends to circle around how others make *us* feel by what they post, tweet, and share. We're puzzled at seeing our friend's bare stomach online as she attempts to sell us her vitamin shake. We're annoyed when an acquaintance shares their opposing political views. We feel lonely or left out when we see that a group of women got together without us. We're envious of another woman's fill-in-the-blank. We huff and puff about all the caps-lock shouting.

Aside from the "Hide" or "Unfollow" button, we have little control over what others post on social media. We do, however, have control over how we let it affect us and, perhaps more importantly, how *we* choose to communicate with others online.

How do we make others feel by what we share? How do we use social media to enhance our friendships rather than hinder them? How can we take something often used as a weapon and turn it instead into a tool for encouraging, blessing, connecting deeply with, honoring, and championing our friends? And are we even asking these questions? If we aren't, we may be flippantly throwing away an opportunity for deepened friendship, because hashtag friendship *can* and *does* enhance real-life friendship if, like everything else in life, we're purposeful with how we use it.

My question to you, after you have scrolled through your Facebook page, is this: Are there friends you enjoy following on social media? Texting with? Receiving comments from?

Now consider why they make hashtag friendship enjoyable for you.

The women you enjoy interacting with by phone and app are likely trying to be purposeful and self-aware in how they use social media. They're probably thinking of social media as a conversation. What kind of person enters a room and starts yelling about their political views, showing pictures of their recent vacation, selling something, or blabbing on about the minutiae of their day? A wise and loving person enters a room and starts a conversation with a question: What did *you* do today? What's going on with *you*?

Social media allows us the opportunity to do this with our real-life friends: share an article with a friend that correlates with the conversation we had yesterday, check in on a sick friend by text, praise a friend and her accomplishments on Facebook, or publicly express gratitude. In other words, a wise woman makes hashtag friendship primarily about others instead of blabbing on about herself.

Good hashtag friends actually consider their friends before posting. *Everyone* has had that social media moment when a posted picture taunts them, seemingly shouting at them that they weren't invited or included in a gathering. This is something I have thought about a lot, because I'm a pastor's wife and most of the ladies in our church are on social media. They see the pictures I post. I'm allowed, of course, to have good friends, but I choose to rarely, if ever, post updates online that highlight who I'm spending time with or who I've invited to certain things. Doing so might hurt feelings. I appreciate when my friends do the same, when they consider the feelings of others as more important than their right to post whatever they want on social media.

Good hashtag friends also resist the urge to make themselves look good. There have been times when something really great happened to me and I want to shout it from the rooftops, but I knew my motivation in sharing it would be pride. I could go the #humblebrag route because I want admiration or respect or some sort of validation, but that's when I try to remember the people in my offline life and think about if I would say in person what I want to post online.

If we aren't being honest and forthright, if we're trying to create an image of something we're not, the friends and potential friends in our offline lives will quickly see through all that, and *we'll eventually hinder our friendships.* The way we handle our online presence can quickly open doors for friendship with others or it can shut them in our face, likely without us even realizing it.

We want to use our online presence for the benefit of others. This is both our goal and our guideline. As applied to Facebook or Twitter, am I generally drawing attention to myself or generally using them as platforms to encourage, champion someone else, say thank you, or connect with women in my real life?

A good hashtag friend knows that life isn't what happens online. Life is happening in real life. Character is proved by what happens in our real, offline lives, not by what we put on Facebook. A wise woman puts far more time into real-life relationships than she does social media and online relationships. A wise woman puts herself face-to-face with her friends so she cannot just speak but also listen and hear and learn and grow. A wise woman, in fact, uses her online presence primarily to connect with her real-life friends.

And also, as we consider hashtag friendship, it might help to return to where we started in this section of the book: "So whatever you wish that others would do to you, do also to them" (Matt. 7:12 ESV).

#Exactly.

PART FIVE

Receiving Friendship

TWENTY-THREE

SOS

Ask for Help

But God has put this Word into the mouth of men in order that it may be communicated to other men. When one person is struck by the Word, he speaks it to others. God has willed that we should seek and find His living Word in the witness of a brother, in the mouth of a man. Therefore, the Christian needs another Christian who speaks God's Word to him. He needs him again and again when he becomes uncertain and discouraged. And that also clarifies the goal of all Christian community: they meet one another as bringers of the message of salvation.

Dietrich Bonhoeffer[1]

On a recent Saturday night, my husband, Kyle, left to officiate a wedding. He planned to pop in, pronounce the couple husband and wife, and pop out quickly so he could get home to finalize his sermon for the following morning. He popped in as planned, but the minute the bride started down the aisle toward her groom, he felt his back seize up. Unable to move or even breathe without excruciating pain, he grimaced his way through the vows. Thankfully, no one noticed, but then again who pays any attention to the officiant at a wedding anyway? He made the marriage pronouncement through gritted teeth before hobbling to his car to return home, knowing that he was experiencing what people refer to as a "back going out."

Kyle shuffled through the door with an almost embarrassed smirk on his face, trying not to move any muscle that didn't need moving.

"What is going on with you?" I asked, trying to reconcile the half smile with the old-man gait.

"Please, just help me sit down," he pleaded, reaching his arm out to use me as a crutch. "My back went out at the wedding."

With my help, he lowered himself onto a kitchen chair and allowed me, as if he were a toddler, to take off his shoes, his coat, and his tie. His embarrassed smirk turned to giggling, a nervous habit of his in any situation in which he's completely helpless.

Google told me I should get my patient flat on the floor, facedown, and ice his back. I retrieved my pink exercise mat from the hall closet and eased him down on it until he was spread out like a stiff board on the living room floor. Only then did I scroll down to read the rest of what WebMD had to say: "and expect the patient to remain motionless for twenty-four hours."

As I read the words out loud, we simultaneously gasped. "Twenty-four hours! But the sermon!" He couldn't even sit up, much less stand and speak.

At the very moment that we were processing what to do, my oldest son moaned from the top of the stairs, "Mom, my stomach hurts." Leaving my husband facedown doing some moaning of his own, I raced upstairs just as my son rushed to the toilet to reveal the remains of his lunch. I helped him to his bed, ensured he was comfortable, and raced back downstairs to nurse my ailing husband.

Thirty minutes later, I heard more unnatural, guttural noises coming from the boys' bathroom. I darted back upstairs, expecting I'd find my oldest son crouched over the toilet but instead finding my *middle* son folded over, looking pale and clammy. Let's just say that he had faced the Sophie's Choice of sickness (sit or kneel?) and had chosen poorly, and there would be buckets of bleach in my immediate future.

Did I mention that I have a third child? Oh yes, yes I do, and he evidently had thoroughly enjoyed close proximity with his brothers that day.

In the following hours, between scrubbing with bleach and laundering loads of sheets, I got Motrin for my husband and held a phone up to his ear as he lay on the floor and conferred with our other pastors about what to do regarding the sermon. Late into the night, I rushed between vomiting sounds and moaning, all the while pleading with God to protect me from getting sick.

At some point, it was decided that another elder would preach and we all finally collapsed from exhaustion, illness, and pain. I sent an SOS text to a few friends that simply said:

Please pray. Everyone's sick. I'm exhausted over here.

The following morning we had multiple offers from friends to bring us food for lunch. Some didn't ask but simply appeared at our door with crackers, soup, and ginger ale, along with well wishes and hugs for me. I wouldn't let them go near my children or even enter the contamination zone called my house, because I wouldn't wish what my kids had on my worst enemy. I stood at the door and received multiple visitors and multiple blessings and sometimes let people in to stare at my husband's back as he lay on the living room floor.

In what we now call the Epic Night of Sickness, I said, "Help!" and my friends were there in an instant. It was a beautiful blessing, a tangible representation of love.

I appreciated the texts, the prayers, and the food so much, but I noticed another encroaching feeling with each bottle of ginger ale presented to me on my front porch, something that felt itchy and restless inside. I came to recognize it as discomfort, because being helpless and needy and smelling like vomit and Lysol in front of others, even close friends, is uncomfortable. I don't want the attention and their sacrifice,

179

because I feel unworthy of them and I know I can't repay the kindness straightaway.

But I had no other options. I couldn't leave my house. I needed the help, so instead of shuffling my feet and averting my eyes from the love and sacrifice, I received it all. I let my friends be my friends.

Resist the Discomfort of Receiving

I decided at one point in my life that, in order to have good friends, it was imperative I set aside once and for all the (laughable) notion that I could get by with always giving but never receiving. In fact, I attribute much of the friendship struggles I experienced in my twenties to my inability or refusal to be helped. I kept myself firmly in the position of giver and need-meeter because receiving required humility and vulnerability that, frankly, I didn't have.

Therein lies the inherent risk. Asking for help from another woman puts us in a vulnerable spot, one where it's quite possible we'll be misunderstood or she'll respond in a truly unhelpful way or we'll be judged as spiritually inferior. But I've found that the reward far outweighs the risk because, aside from intentional vulnerability, relying on the help of friends is one of the greatest catalysts for deepening friendship.

I have a friend who holds her cards close to her chest. If something is going on with her, not a soul knows about it. After a few times of finding out after the fact that she had encountered some bumps in the road and had not asked me for physical help or even prayer, I began to question whether she really considered me her friend. I felt pretty certain that she did, but her lack of vulnerability and dependence on me have made it difficult for us to deepen our friendship. The times she has let me in and let me serve her in some way, I've been met with profuse apology, as if it's a burden or a bother. I wish I could get across to her that I love her and that it's my joy and honor to serve her. I wish I could tell her that it's a blessing to me to be invited into the private and personal areas of her life. I want to help her when she needs it. It's how I can fulfill the "one anothers" in Scripture, and I don't want to be denied that opportunity, especially with someone I consider a friend.

I see my old self in her, the self who felt unworthy and, honestly, unwilling to receive from others. I noticed over time in my own life that other women only tried to push through that prideful wall for so long. Because I didn't ask for help from others, because I was only comfortable being a giver, I came across as plastic, as if I had it all together and didn't need anything. Now I see what they saw, and I know they knew I either wasn't being real about my life or wasn't a person they could be real with. They likely assumed I was not someone who could relate to any neediness they might have, so my friendships were unable to deepen.

I'm not sure that discomfort in receiving ever truly goes away for any of us, but it's something we're going to have to work through if we want to have good friends. Because friendship is about mutuality. I want to love my friends by giving to them, and I have to believe they feel the same way. And you know what? I don't want any of my friends to take away my opportunity to bless and serve and give to them. Why would I take away their opportunity to do the same for me? I certainly don't want to negate what they do give by profusely apologizing or trying to repay them or evaluating what they've done. That's not friendship. That's business or charity or something else entirely, something lacking Holy Spirit–infused intimacy.

Outside Help for Inside Struggles

I'm far past the discomfort of asking for help from my friends regarding my physical needs, but I'm still learning to move past the discomfort of asking for help with my emotional and spiritual needs. Just recently, in fact, God initiated a work in my life that began with his discipline. As I sorted through what he was trying to say to me, I found too much fog and confusion to think clearly on my own. I needed outside help, so I asked for my closest friends to enter in.

I asked for their prayers. I told them I wasn't doing well. I explained that I wasn't even sure what was going on with me but that I felt intense spiritual oppression. I told them what the Lord had convicted me of and how, after that, I'd felt all tangled up in my mind. I told them I felt despair and how all I knew to do was to wait on the Lord and ask people to pray for me.

My friends came running. They offered time, listening ears, biblical truth, words of encouragement, prayers, and, in all these things, important space for me to not be OK until I really was. In many of my conversations with them I was a blubbering mess, but they patiently helped me sort through my thoughts and emotions until I came to somewhat of a conclusion as to what the Lord was doing.

Frankly, it was uncomfortable for me to invite them into my mess. It was uncomfortable for me to not be OK in full view of other women. It was uncomfortable revealing my deepest thoughts, many of them sinful. But in intentional receiving from godly women there is great benefit and reward, and I was just such a beneficiary. The benefits? Wise counsel and the ministry of the body of Christ. The rewards? Deepening friendship and a profound commitment to go and do likewise for others.

I'm not saying that we should be constantly needy and clingy and expect everyone to come running all the time. Biblical dependence and reliance on others in friendship are such that, after we've received them, they cause us to respond with gratitude to God that he would give us help through others. In the end, this is a reliance on the Lord, a trust that he will use his church to minister to us in the way he ordains.

We are to be those ministers, yes, but we're also to position ourselves as humble receivers. And positioning usually means asking.

Ask for wisdom from an older and more experienced woman regarding your work, marriage, or children.

Ask a friend to pray for you.

Ask for feedback from a wise friend regarding what you're struggling through.

Just ask, even if it's through tears and sweat and bleach and lying facedown on the living room floor.

TWENTY-FOUR

Heed

Embrace Correction

The sweetness of a friend comes from his earnest counsel.

Proverbs 27:9 ESV

Friends are fun. I love grabbing a meal or going for a walk with a friend. I love laughing with a friend. I love gathering my friends together and experiencing life with them.

Friendships among Christians are even more fun, in my opinion, because they occur between two people who are savoring the same discovered treasure: If God is for us—and he is—who can be against us? The friendship of God, then, makes friendship between Christians the most joyful, peaceful, and stable kind of friendship, because it ultimately reflects the delighted communion of the Father, the Son, and the Holy Spirit and God's love for us. What a pleasure it is to be in the company of other beloveds as we entrust our hearts to him.

However, God has added an ingredient to friendship that makes it distinctly Christian and that, by all accounts, is not fun but in the end is for our benefit and even for our delight.

This ingredient is suffering.

In other words, Christian friendship is marked by a willingness to lovingly wound a friend for her eventual growth, which we've already discussed, and a willingness to *receive* the faithful wounds of a friend for *our* eventual growth.

Christian friendship is like old-fashioned laundering. We are wrung out in the wash through the faithful twisting, scrubbing, and squeezing of a friend, because she sees and desires the end of it all: our purity. She wants the best for us.

So, yes, friends are for fun.

But they are also for our sanctification.

After hearing a talk on handling conflict, one friend and I were discussing how most people try to avoid conflict altogether but that doing so creates a sense of fake peace.

I said, "It made me realize that I really *do* want to handle conflict well. I really *do* want to know when I've hurt my friends, because I don't want there to be anything between us."

She wrinkled up her nose, hesitated for a second, and said, "Well, now that you mention it . . ."

And suddenly I wasn't so sure.

Help for Healing

As I walked through my season of confusion this past fall and called in the help of my friends, I realized that the sin God was revealing in my heart was likely affecting my friendships in ways to which I'd been blind. I could only be sure by actually confessing my sin to them and asking them for forgiveness and feedback. I needed my friends to help me see myself in ways I couldn't get an angle on by myself.

Talk about scary.

I wasn't sure I could do it, because I felt bent over and fragile. What if their responses were like bludgeons to my knees? Why would I hand them the weapons to hurt me?

But I held tightly to a few things I knew to be true. One, the Lord was nudging me toward them in a way I couldn't ignore. Two, I knew I needed the ministry of my friends. Three, I trusted the wisdom and love of my friends. They weren't knee-bludgeoners. They weren't eager to wield weapons against me. And four, hope pointed toward the healing that stood waiting for me on the other side of these difficult conversations. I could practically touch it.

So I had the conversations.

I told them, one by one, about the ugly stuff in my heart, and then I asked them, "What is it like to be friends with me? How have these things I'm sharing affected our friendship?"

No one ran screaming from the room. No one gasped in shock and horror. No one took up a weapon against me. But the conversations were excruciatingly painful nonetheless. It was agonizing to admit my thoughts and heart's motivations, even to loving friends. And even though I knew it was right and true, it was just as excruciatingly painful to hear them confirm how they'd seen my thoughts and motivations spill over into my actions and how that had made them feel.

I found out pretty quickly why God had nudged me toward these friends with my specific questions. Without knowing what my other friends were saying, each gave basically the same answers to my questions. It was clear what God wanted to point out.

The pain came not from their responses but from seeing myself and my sin so clearly. However, knowing I was in pain, each in turn began building me back up with truth from Scripture. They reminded me I always have an avenue to deal with my sin—that I can confess and repent and be cleansed by the Lord. They told me they forgave me. They told me God would help me change. They told me they loved me and would walk with me through the process.

I felt as if each of them was poking around in an open wound, searching for what needed to be removed in order that the wound might heal, or as if I were the dirty laundry that was being scrubbed hard in order for stains to be removed.

They gave me hope that healing and cleansing could actually come.

Faithless or Faithful?

A few times in my conversations, however, I bristled internally at my friends' responses. I wanted to excuse that one thing or explain that other thing away. I wanted to defend myself. I wanted to say, "You see, this is why that is," or perhaps, "Could we just not go there?"

But I remembered what I'd read in Proverbs a few months prior, that a faithful friend wounds in order that healing may happen. I remembered how I had tried to do this myself with my friends. A faithful friend doesn't avoid the hard things; in fact, she loves so much that she's willing to experience wounding herself—the self-inflicted pain of knowing you've said a difficult thing that will temporarily wound.

A faithless friend can't do that. A faithless friend loves herself and her own comfort more than she loves others. A faithless friend allows us to hurt ourselves and others rather than do the difficult work of stopping us in our tracks.

My friends were of the faithful variety, and I would be wise, I reminded myself, to receive their ministry. That's another lesson Proverbs wants to teach: "He who regards a rebuke will be honored," and "The ear that hears the rebukes of life will abide among the wise" (Prov. 13:18; 15:31). We are wise to accept wounds from a friend.

A faithless friend chooses passivity when a hard word is needed, but I would be just as faithless of a friend to refuse to *heed* a hard word. So instead of bristling or explaining away, I chose to listen closely, to digest carefully the wisdom my friends were presenting to me. Their words were wounds meant to usher me toward healing, and they found their mark.

At other times in my life, the faithful wounds of a friend have come unexpectedly and unrequested. In other words, I wasn't prepared to receive them, and in those moments the temptation toward panic, anger, or defensiveness proved far greater than when I'd asked for them.

Unexpected wounds can hurt more, although they often are similarly motivated by a friend's desire for reconciliation or for our growth, and it's important we decide in advance how we'll respond when they come. I know myself and know how defensive and stubborn I can be, so I've committed to myself that I will listen and receive what comes my way without acting put-upon or reflexively trying to explain myself.

But then there is something else I'm committed to doing, because sometimes people say things and they're not wounds from a faithful friend; they are simply wounds. I haven't always known how to distinguish the two or even that I should distinguish the two, but I know myself and I know that I'm far too sensitive to every word spoken to me. One wound, even from a friend, and I suddenly berate myself that I've been a fool before all the world. So I've committed that I will listen and receive and then, as soon as I can get alone, I will place all the words I've received before the Lord. I will ask for his eyes and his Spirit's help as I turn them over and inspect them. Will he gently confirm the accuracy of the words I've heard? Are there some inaccuracies to the wound that I am released to set aside? What, if anything, am I to change or to do to seek reconciliation or make things right?

And are these actually wounds from a friend? Are they from someone who knows me, loves me, and is approaching me under the Holy Spirit's leading because they want the best for me? If so, I need to seriously consider everything they've said. But sometimes I know right away that this person isn't necessarily a friend. She doesn't know me as well as others or she may not know the specific situation fully. I still take the things she said to the Lord, because there is generally a nugget of truth I can digest. What perspective can the Lord give me on the person who has come to me? How might that perspective give me compassion for her and the hurts she has experienced from me or from others? And again, what, if anything, am I to do with her words?

When my friend Jessica was over one day, she asked an innocent question that made me want to explode inside. She didn't know it—and I didn't even know it, to tell you the truth—but she touched on something that had been brewing in my heart. Ugly stuff, like pride and spitefulness, if you really want to know, and lots of other things unbecoming to a follower of Christ. Just one simple question—and an unknowing one at that—and God himself poked at something I'd have preferred to keep hidden. As if I was hiding it from him.

Of course, seeing my reaction, she probed in her quiet, firm way, and her words that day set me off on a course of confession and repentance, and then more confession and repentance, and eventually needed reconciliation with someone in my life.

It started with one simple question, her deep and abiding love for the Lord and for me, and a few well-placed words.

God made it obvious: *This is from me. Listen and receive.*

Wounds from a friend—faithful indeed.

TWENTY-FIVE

Savor

Unwrap Imperfect Gifts with Gratefulness

My friends have come to me unsought. The great God gave them to me.

Ralph Waldo Emerson[1]

Lately I'm realizing how I'm an expert at taking the beautiful blessings of life and turning them into cheerless burdens. I can find a way to complain about some of the most mysteriously rich treasures of life, treasures that have so blatantly come from God's hand.

I'm a delight to be around, I'm sure.

It's true that gifts from God aren't always easy to receive. Well, I take that back. Most are easy to receive but almost all are difficult to steward. God's all, *Here's a little baby who will need nurture and care for the rest of his life! You'll rejoice when he rejoices but you'll also suffer when he suffers. And sometimes he will break your heart. Enjoy!*

And that just sort of applies to everything.

With friends, it's more like, *Here's a friend you won't recognize as a friend right away. After a few years of occasionally having good conversations while your children are running laps around both of you, you'll realize she's a friend you cherish. She will unintentionally hurt you sometimes and forget your birthday and one day she will move away. She will challenge you in good and hard ways. You will laugh with her until you think you're going to pee in your pants. She will press into things that you'd prefer to keep hidden, but I will use her to help you grow. Enjoy!*

Gifts from God aren't like finding a toy under the Christmas tree; they typically aren't as obvious as a wrapped gift, and they require thought and purposefulness and work and obedience. They require us to choose to acknowledge them as gifts or else they quickly become frustrations and we quickly become complainers.

We don't like things to be hard; let's just be honest. Sometimes I cross my arms and think/pray, *And how is it again that this relationship is a good gift from you?* I like toy-gifts, not work-gifts, because I like gifts of the comfortable, me-centered variety.

But I'm starting to notice that God-gifts take awhile to unwrap.

It's almost like we want to tally what we've received, set it aside in a pile that we protect, and greedily seek something more, something better, rather than savoring the actual gifts and the love that motivated the Giver.

Receive Friendship Wisely

It seems to me that there is a foolish way to receive a gift—a childish way—and then there is a wise way.

I noticed as a child that, when the Christmas presents were passed out, my grandparents set theirs aside, preferring to open their gifts after everyone else. They typically had a small stack of gifts, so in my childish thinking I assumed they were slightly disappointed and wanted to make their gift-opening time last. But as I got older, I realized I had it all wrong. They set their gifts aside because they enjoyed watching everyone else open their gifts. They wanted to see the doll I received and the toy my sister opened and, mostly, they wanted to see our joy. After all us kids had torn through our presents, we'd watch as they took their turn. They opened each one slowly and took time to look at each gift and talk with the gift-giver about it, in a savoring kind of way.

This now seems very wise to me, and not just because they extended the gift-opening time. It seems wise because it wasn't about what might come next but about what they had already received.

If this is the wise way to receive gifts—to savor, to know that a gift takes time to unwrap and to come to its fullest giving—it seems to me that this would also be the wisest way for me to receive the gift of friendship. I need to give friendships time to develop, to let them marinate, to enjoy moments when friends are sharing themselves with me, to enjoy the One who has put us together. It is no coincidence where I am in life. God has chosen it for me. And it is no coincidence who is beside me. To think of the intricate threads in the tapestry of my life is to consider the carefulness God has shown in giving me my friends.

I turn these blessings into complaints and disappointment because I don't savor, I know I don't. I'm kid-greedy, already moving on, already thinking, *OK, who's next?* or *What's missing?* or *What have I not received yet from my friendships that I want?*

But what if I'm missing what's next? What if the "next" is already in my life? What if I'm complaining about the work of the unwrapping process—all the work that goes into developing and maintaining friendships—and it's keeping me from the joy of this exact slice of life that God himself has given me?

Receive Friendship with Thanksgiving

There can be no doubt: God has given us friends. He has given us the church. He has given us relationships for fun and for sanctification and to help us live wise lives. The gifts are all around us, if we have eyes to see and savor them.

If you're like me, more often than not you're considering the holes in your life. Perhaps you're new to your town and haven't made any friends to speak of. Perhaps you're feeling frustrated with your current church situation. Perhaps you've just been on Instagram and are feeling left out of the mom circle around you. There don't appear to be gifts all around you, just frustrations and longings.

But I want you to imagine your current life without friends—anyone on the spectrum from acquaintances to lifelong friends. Imagine that you didn't ever meet that girl in the dorm during college or the high school classmate who told you about Jesus. Imagine never knowing your co-worker or the girl in your small group at church. Imagine never having had that family in your home for dinner or not being invited to that birthday party. Imagine living the Christian life without the church and its truth-teaching; worship-singing; and people praying, serving, and giving. In other words, imagine moving through life solitarily. When life-altering decisions have to be made, you're on your own. When you need support, you have no one to whom you can turn. When you need a good laugh, you have no one to laugh with. A solitary life would be a life of no shared burdens and no shared companionship. It would be heavier and less de-lightful, and how would you see anything but your own small perspective?

What a wonder that God has given us other people and that some of those people become dear friends! What a gift that we get to live life alongside others! Friendship is truly one of the sweetest gifts in life.

My biggest struggles in friendship, whether loneliness or unmet expectations or hurts, have generally filtered through a belief that I'm entitled to have it in the exact form I want it. The biggest boon to my friendships, however, has been an attitude of receptive thanksgiving for what is right in front of me.

This has proven to be a wise way of unwrapping.

Give It Time

Have you ever had the experience of excitedly planning a meeting with someone you want to get to know and then, when you finally got to-gether, you left feeling disappointed because she didn't ask you any ques-tions or things just seemed a bit off? Those are moments when we grow easily discouraged and want to give up on that person or on initiating with others. But those are the exact moments that call for thanksgiving, because they are opportunities to look for the gift in that person. Were they everything you hoped they'd be? Probably not. For that matter, were you everything they hoped you'd be? Probably not. But what about the nugget of hard-won wisdom she shared with you? What about the fact that she graciously paid for your tea? What does it mean that she gave up her lunch break or switched around her work schedule so she could get together with you? What about the way she asked you those questions or spoke one simple word of encouragement? Did you have something in common? Did she allow you into her life at all?

Dietrich Bonhoeffer once again helps set us straight:

> Because God has already laid the only foundation of our fellow-ship, because God has bound us together in one body with other Christians in Jesus Christ, long before we entered into common life with them, we enter into that common life not as demanders but as thankful recipients. . . . We do not complain of what God does not give us; we rather thank God for what He does give us daily. . . . If we do not give thanks daily for the Christian fellowship in which we have been placed, even where there is no great experience, no discoverable riches, but much weakness, small faith, and difficulty; if on the contrary, we only keep complaining to God that everything is so paltry and petty, so far from what we expected, then we hinder God from letting our fellowship grow according to the measure and riches which are there for us all in Jesus Christ.[2]

In other words, we should view friendship as a gift and humbly acknowledge that the unwrapping will take time. It will take starts and stops. It will take space and grace. Let us not, in our wish-dream fantasies or our entitlement or our expectations of perfection, crush what God intended as a delicate gift to slow-open.

To Savor Is to Experience Joy

My grandparents have found the secret: there is joy in savoring. Savoring includes the initial delight at having discovered something rare and sweet and the subsequent treasuring of such a gift over time. Savoring is what fuels gratefulness.

So instead of complaining about what we don't have in regard to friendship, let us savor what we do have, even the moments or seasons of loneliness that cause us to turn to the Lord as our only true companion. Our every need is met in him. Let us celebrate every little outpouring of friendship, no matter how small or how slow to start it is. Let us consider what a blessing it is to *give* friendship to others, to walk alongside them in their joys and sorrows. Let us also rejoice that we get to see God at work in our friends.

Savoring a gift always turns our eyes toward the One who gave it. There is nothing in the world like spending time with another person who, when we leave them, makes us feel we cannot help but turn to worship God.

C. S. Lewis puts it this way:

> For a Christian there are, strictly speaking, no chances. A secret Master of Ceremonies has been at work. Christ, who said to the disciples "Ye have not chosen me, but I have chosen you," can truly say to every group of Christian friends "You have not chosen one another but I have chosen you for one another." The Friendship is not a reward for our discrimination and good taste in finding one another out. It is the instrument by which God reveals to each the beauties of all the others. . . . They are, like all beauties, derived from Him, and then, in a good Friendship, increased by Him through the Friendship itself, so that it is His instrument for creating as well as for revealing.[3]

We receive a friend—new or old—as we do a gift, a discovered treasure: with thanksgiving.

I imagine my Father God is much like my grandparents at Christmas. As all grandparents do, he's gone *way* overboard in the gift department. He's not sitting in the corner, focused on his presents, looking to be served. He's looking over to see if I've started to open *that* present, the one he picked out just for me. And, like any gift-giver, he simply wants me to enjoy it and then run to thank him. This gift may challenge me a little bit—he knows that—but he's given me this gift after careful deliberation and with so much love. He also knows that part of the joy of receiving the gift is the thought, purposefulness, work, and obedience it will require of me.

Sometimes, when I'm grumpy and I know I'm not savoring the gifts right in front of me, when I'm turning blessings into burdens, I do this little trick in which I imagine myself in the future without the friends I have today. I imagine how I would feel if I were unable to see them or if we moved away. I think about not having the people who make up our church in my life and about never knowing my lifelong friends, and it helps me see quickly and clearly that what I think I lack is nothing at all to complain about. I have my "what next" right in front of me, and they are all blessings, no matter how imperfect they are or how imperfect a friend I am.

When I do my little trick, I just sit with them, tearing off a little more wrapping paper, savoring. They aren't burdens any longer, as if they ever were. They are blessings—my blessings—and I can't help but run to my Father to say thank you.

Conclusion

The Sweetest Thing

At this feast it is He who has spread the board and it is He who has chosen the guests. It is He, we may dare to hope, who sometimes does, and always should, preside. Let us not reckon without our Host.

C. S. Lewis[1]

When our friend Sara moved away in eighth grade, Jo and I sang together at the evening church service in her honor. We had no problem at all deciding on the song: Michael W. Smith's "Friends." We did, however, have an actual *singing* problem, on account of neither of us could sing on pitch. That night, we also had trouble remembering the lyrics a few times during the song, which we stealthily covered over by glancing side-eye at each other, giggling into the microphone, and then coming in loud and strong with the well-trod chorus: "Friends are friends forever / If the Lord's the Lord of them."[2]

Afterward I probably went home and ate a sandwich and watched *Beverly Hills, 90210* on the VCR, not all that concerned about being separated from Sara by a few states. I would miss her, of course, but

I was in eighth grade, and when you're in eighth grade the long-term gravity of most situations is difficult to grasp. No thought goes beyond the next school year, when your life changes according to your locker location and class schedule. Your optimism and hope concerning the future stretch for miles, so you don't necessarily feel this great longing for things to be made right or for there to be no more loss or separation. I wasn't so sure that I'd *really* be friends forever with anyone. Actually, I was pretty certain at that age that I'd be forever young and invincible and, if you want to know the truth, I wasn't all that concerned with anyone else but myself and whether my peacock shirt was clean for the following school day.

What I thought was true when I was young has turned farcical, and what I thought could never happen has actually happened. Perky optimism has gotten its pretty little head trampled on a bit. As I've gotten older and experienced separation from friends through distance or death, not to mention all the dark and difficult arrows that pierce us in this life, one thing has come squarely into view as deeply, profoundly true: we are all hurtling toward eternity, and eternity is, well, eternal. Now I think far more about what is beyond today and far less about the cares of this world.

It seems the Michael W. Smith song Jo and I sang in eighth grade may not have been so idealistic after all. Cheesy and sappy, yes, but in some ways it was a strong theological treatise on friendship. Friends really *are* friends forever if the Lord is the Lord of them. That's no joke.

I always imagine heaven as a great big dinner party—not too fancy, full of laughter and warmth and satisfying food. I imagine our celebratory God at the head of the table, and although in my imagination I can't stop looking at him and taking in his every word, sometimes I remember that there are others sitting beside me and I turn to look at them too.

They are my friends. Sara and Jo. Anne and Natalie, the friends I made in college. Ashley, Jamee, and Niki from our adult years in Texas. My beloved friends from Charlottesville and everyone spread across the globe to whom I send Christmas cards. These women will sit at the table with me forever. I love that so much, because I don't get to see these women as much as I'd like and some, like Claire, I won't see again until we are seated for that dinner party in heaven.

Friends are but one reason—and an important one at that—why I've developed a strong desire to be in God's presence in heaven. The longing for him, for faith to be made sight, and for everything to be made beautiful and right has become like a low-grade fever in my heart. I want to be made well but all I can do about it is to give it time, slow-open what I have now, and medicate my fever with faith.

Aside from seeing God face-to-face, I most look forward to right relationships with others, especially these friends I've had throughout my life. We will relate to one another without jealousy, misunderstanding, separation, or comparison. Sin will not blind us to the way we wound one another, nor will it mar our words and interactions. We will love one another perfectly. Perhaps best of all, we will have unlimited time together; death and physical separation will not be able to take us from one another ever again.

Who knew that Michael W. Smith was so prophetic?

The Future and the Present

Our friendships point to a different time, to something more. They pull us outward to where we can see a greater picture and then draw us back in close to work at them persistently and purposefully in our everyday lives. Our faith tells us that our wish-dream will be so, that there will be a time when our friendship-longing will be fulfilled. We will be satisfied and at peace with one another, free of shaming and blaming, in right relationship with one another and with God, confident in our affinity and affection, because we will be satisfied in God.

And so, having seen the big picture of time, we're tugged back to the present day as though through a small portal. What do we have now in this gift called friendship? We have the gospel, our hope of what once was and what is to come. This gospel gives us the ability, as we wait, to practice what we'll do in perpetuity and to, in the present tense, draw toward one another in imitation of how Christ has drawn near to us. With

reconciliation

forgiveness

pursuit

sacrificial love

help

delight

truth

grace

compassion

probing questions

affection

understanding

friendship

May our friendships in the present day be received as gifts from God for us—but may they not be *only* for us. May they be signposts, guiding any who will stop and seek directions toward what our hearts innately crave most, pointing the seeker toward a Person and a place where all longings will be longings no more. For it is only in true Christian friendship that two people who are different in every way possible— race, background, language, personality, socioeconomic level—can love like this. As Tim Keller has said, "In the gospel . . . Jesus Christ is breaking into the lives of all kinds of people. . . . Suddenly . . . you find other people who otherwise are different in every other way, except the deepest passion of their life is to love Jesus Christ. . . . When I find somebody whose deepest affinity is my deepest affinity . . . think of the potential. Christian friendships are so radical and so exhilarating and so enriching."[3]

They shall know us by our love. And they shall know him too.

It follows, then, that friendship is worth the effort.

It's worth it to leave your wounded isolation and try again. It's worth it to forgive a sister. It's worth it to give your time and energy to your friendships. It's worth it to push through the awkward. It's worth it to love and serve and seek to understand.

We're not at the supper table yet, and it's going to be a long, arduous journey to get there. By enduring with one another and bearing with one another, by being willing to walk through the gore of life and hold our friends' fragile stories close to ourselves while simultaneously offering them hope, by receiving wounding kisses from a faithful friend, we are essentially linking arms and journeying toward that table together.

When we sit side by side at the supper table, we will be celebrating that, by God's grace, we made it to our destination. We made it because of Christ, we made it with the help of our friends, and we made it together.

This is why friendship is worth it: because it is something that will continue forever in heaven.

Sara moved away in eighth grade, and I don't know her anymore, unless you count reading her updates on Facebook.

But I will know her again.

Claire died, and I can't ask her any of my pressing questions about marriage and parenting.

But I will talk to her again.

All the friends in my life—the one I'll meet for coffee this afternoon, those I'll see on my annual trek home this summer, and all those in between—I will know and be known by them not just again but perfectly.

Because (sing with me now!) friends are friends forever if the Lord's the Lord of them.

Acknowledgments

*J*o, you taught me everything I know about friendship and you continue to teach me. Thirty years and counting.

Girls' weekend girls, I love what we have.

Susan, Marylyn, Nikki, Emily, and Amy, thank you for cheering me on, valuing my written words, praying for me, and helping me sort through my thoughts for this book. I love being friends with each of you.

Karen Roland, Emily Coleman, Lacy Nuckols, Saundra Hutchison, Carri Drake, Amanda Scott, Kate Richardson, and Amy Eckert, that evening in my living room launched this book. Thank you for sharing your friendship stories and your wisdom with me and with each other. (Nikki Hart and Melanie Jones, thank you both for chiming in by email.)

Susan Hamil, Jenny Chen, Aimee Saunders, Melissa Barrow, Kate Richardson, Ishan Williams, Jessica Brumbelow, and Kay and Kenny Fulmer, thank you for letting me use your stories. Thank you even more for teaching me through them.

Claire, you always believed there would be more books. Thank you for that. I miss you. Improbably, I feel as if I know you more now through your beloved family. DeLauras, I love you all.

I obviously have resonated deeply with Dietrich Bonhoeffer's thoughts about Christian community in his book *Life Together*. I'm indebted to his work and am thankful for how his words changed my perspective on friendship.

Andrew Wolgemuth, thank you for coming alongside me and this project with wisdom and enthusiasm.

To the entire Baker Books team, thanks for having me! I have thoroughly enjoyed working with each of you. Rebekah Guzman, thank you especially for your thoughtful editing and encouragement and for championing my work. You make me believe I am a real writer.

Nicci Jordan Hubert, thank you for your thoughtful editing. Twice!

To the people of Charlottesville Community Church, I'm grateful to God for forming our church the way he has. You are the most loving, hospitable, prayerful, servant-hearted people I've known. In my life, I've learned the most about friendship in the years CCC has existed because of each of you and your commitment to the Lord, to the gospel, and to people. Thank you for loving me, honoring Kyle, and caring for my children. Thank you for being patient with me, challenging me, and giving me grace to learn and grow. I absolutely love being your pastor's wife.

To my parents, Larry and Dana Fleming, thank you for setting an example for me in so many ways, but especially in the area of generosity in friendship.

Kyle, you are my favorite person. You are such an incredible man, and I thank God that I get to be your wife. Thank you for your never-ending support and encouragement in all areas of my life, especially in my writing. I couldn't do this without you. I love you.

To my boys, you bring me joy! I love watching you grow up into young men. My prayer for each of you is that you will enjoy deep and abiding friendships in your life. You are well on your way.

Father God, a simple thank-you is not potent enough to convey how I feel about how you've befriended me through Christ. I have found the most valuable treasure. Thank you for showing me what love is and being patient with me as I learn to love like you. Thank you also for allowing me the opportunity to write. I pray it honors you.

Questions for Friends to Discuss Together

Part 1: A New Vision for Friendship

Chapter 1: When Did Friendship Become Such a Struggle?

1. In your friendships, do you find yourself wishing for the "way it was"?

2. Are your "way it was" friendships a standard you measure adult friendships by? How is that helping or hindering your current friendships or attempts at friendships?

3. Christine mentions examples and lessons she picked up in her childhood that have served her well. What are helpful lessons you learned about friendship in your younger years?

Chapter 2: The Dreams We Have for Friendship

1. What is your wish-dream regarding friendship?

2. As God has graciously shattered your wish-dream, how have you responded? Have you isolated yourself, grown bitter, or continued to hold an unattainable standard over other women?

3. How is your wish-dream hurting you and others?

4. How can we distinguish between a wish-dream and godly desires for friendship?

Chapter 3: How God Gives Friendship

1. How have you experienced the friendship of God?

2. Have you ever tried to make friends replacements for God?

3. How do our instinctual, feelings-oriented ways of friendship sometimes differ from the imperatives of Scripture?

4. How does your perspective of friendship need to change in order for it to align with God's plan for friendship?

Chapter 4: Messy Beautiful Friendship

1. Who are the people God has placed in your life? Are you quick to overlook some women as possible friends because they are not whom you envisioned as friends?

2. Do you view friendship as a means of sanctification?

3. How have you avoided God's specific work of sanctification in your life through friendship?

4. Christine defines Christian friendship as birthed out of a security in God, where we can love without expectation of return. How can we develop that ability?

5. How do you need to persevere in your friendships right now?

Part 2: Threats to Friendship

Chapter 5: Fear of Being Burned

1. Christine says that friendship must begin with a belief that in this world we will have trouble. How has believing friendship should be trouble-free affected you?

2. How have you been hurt in friendship? How has that hurt fed your fear of close relationships?

3. Are you afraid of facing conflict head-on? Why or why not?

4. What does God's Word say about your specific fears?

Chapter 6: Ashes of Insecurity

1. Do you tend to view women according to their primary identity—a new creation in Christ—or their secondary identities? If secondary, why do you tend to do this?

2. Christine shared her assumptions about what Aimee thought of her. How do our assumptions result in hurting others?

3. Read the questions we ask ourselves about relationships: *Do these people like me? Can I make them like me? Will they accept me? Will they love me? What will they give me? What are they expecting from me? Will they hurt me?* How can we transform our thoughts from these to a biblical perspective on others—*How can I serve this person? How can I bless this person? What can I learn from this person?*

4. Are you being drawn into an "Inner Ring" where "we" are one thing and "they" another?

5. Is there someone you've hurt with whom you need to pursue reconciliation?

Chapter 7: Kindling for the Campfire

1. When it comes to initiating with other women, are you a sitter or a seeker?

2. Do you have to have an outgoing personality to be an initiator? Why or why not? What are ways all types of personalities can seek the good of other women?

3. What is the biblical motivation for seeking to understand others or show generosity toward them? Is it to win friends?

4. Are we entitled to or guaranteed friends if we're initiative-takers? Why or why not? Why is entitlement a threat to friendship?

Chapter 8: The Spark

1. Why is an unwillingness to be vulnerable a hindrance to deep friendship?

2. What is the difference between wise and unwise vulnerability?

3. Do you find vulnerability risky? Why or why not?

4. If you find vulnerability difficult, what steps can you take to reveal yourself more to wise women?

5. Has anyone ever been vulnerable with you about their sin? What did you learn through that about the gospel? What did that do to your relationship?

6. How can you help cultivate a safe atmosphere for vulnerability in your friendships and in your church?

Part 3: Discovering and Deepening Friendship

Chapter 9: Be Kevin Bacon

1. Are you a person who generally goes toward others in friendship or do you wait for people to come to you?

2. Christine says we are often separated from one another by an unwillingness to be uncomfortable. Do you agree? Why or why not?

3. What does the biblical command to love one another have to do with being willing to push through awkwardness?

4. What can you do today to initiate connection with an acquaintance or friend?

Chapter 10: Back Doors

1. What excuses keep us from inviting other women into our homes?

2. Why are our homes such helpful tools for discovering and deepening friendship?

3. How does the worldly idea of hospitality sometimes hinder our attempts at friendship?

4. What is a biblical definition of hospitality?

5. What is one way you want to grow in extending hospitality to other women?

Chapter 11: No Makeup

1. When have you been the beneficiary of someone else's story? When have you been comforted by someone who's been comforted by God, as 2 Corinthians describes?

2. What are your stories? What has God done in your life? How can you share those stories with other women?

3. How are our stories tools for discovering and deepening friendship?

Chapter 12: Dance Card

1. Is your dance card too full for friendship? If so, why? Is it your own doing, or has God purposefully filled it in this season?

2. Christine spoke of "doing what you have to do" in order to have time for friends. If you're struggling to find time for friendship, what are new and different ways you can approach it? What sacrifice or commitment will this require from you?

3. Have you been frustrated by a friend's limitations or lack of time for friendship? How can you respond graciously to their limits?

Chapter 13: Friend Magnet

1. Do you know women who seem to be friend magnets? As you've observed them interacting with other people, what is it about them that is so attractive?

2. What would our interactions look like if we were women who entered a room with a "There *you* are!" instead of a "Here *I* am!"?

3. What does it mean to honor others?

4. Christine says that part of honoring others is connecting others. What practical steps can you take to connect women with one another?

5. Are there any around you who are on the outside, new, or marginalized? How will you honor these women?

Chapter 14: Naming

1. According to the reflection questions given in the chapter, who are your people?

2. Are they people who point you to Christ? If so, thank God for them.

3. Are you stewarding those relationships well? If not, what do you need to do differently?

Part 4: Being a Friend

Chapter 15: Back and Forth

1. The Bible says we should think about how we want to be treated and then do that for others. How do you want to be treated in conversations with friends?

2. Christine offered a question that is helpful in most situations: "Would you tell me more?" What are questions you've found helpful in deepening friendship?

3. There is such a thing as asking too many questions. How can we distinguish between being a good question-asker and a busybody?

4. Do you struggle with repeating what your friends have told you in confidence? How has this hurt your friendships? What have you learned from these past mistakes?

Chapter 16: Honey

1. What one word would you choose to describe your speech?

2. How have the words of your friends impacted you for the better or for the worse?

3. Christine says that in order for our words to be sweet, we must first be committed to consistently seeking and savoring the Scriptures. Why is that important? Are you committed to seeking and savoring Christ in Scripture?

4. How do our words reflect our future resurrection in Christ?

5. If you're discussing this with friends, use your words now to encourage them. Tell them how you see God at work in their lives.

Chapter 17: What Friends Are For

1. Watching our friends struggle or walk through pain is extremely difficult to do. Christine mentioned her own nervousness and fear of saying the wrong thing. What is your typical response when a friend is hurting?

2. Christine says that walking through adversity with a friend ultimately anchors us to God. Have you experienced this? What did you learn about God in your friend's adversity?

3. How could it be ultimately joyful to walk with someone in their pain?

4. What do Job's friends teach us about what to do and what not to do in response to a friend's adversity?

Chapter 18: One Word

1. Are you a "fixer"? How can being a fixer sometimes compound our friends' painful circumstances?

2. How is it helpful to remember that God stands between us and our friends? That we don't have to try to be their Christ?

3. What is the difference between being merciful and empathetic and entering a friend's pain and trying to be their Christ?

4. Might you consider praying one word for your friends this month or this year? What word would you choose for each of them?

Chapter 19: Room to Breathe

1. It is not always wrong to go to our friends for help or counsel. How do we know when we've crossed the line and are looking for our friends to meet needs only God can meet?

2. How does expecting our friends to be Christ for us lead to conflict? What else does it lead to?

3. Have you ever had a friendship in which you felt unrealistic expectations were being placed on you? How can we respond to these kinds of relationships in an honoring way?

4. What does it mean to bear with one another in friendship?

Chapter 20: Faithful Wounds

1. Have you ever confronted a friend? What was the result? What did you learn from the experience?

2. Is it loving to confront someone we love regarding their sin? Why or why not?

3. Christine gave methodical steps for confrontation. What would you add to these steps, if anything?

4. Why must we be ready and willing to confess our own sins in the midst of confrontation?

Chapter 21: Homesick

1. Do you have friends who aren't Christians? How are you trying to display the beauty of the gospel to them?

2. What can sometimes make friendship with non-Christians more challenging? How are you trying to overcome those challenges?

3. Christine said that, after she complained to her friend, she realized that what sets her apart from unbelieving friends is going to be heart characteristics like joy and gratefulness. Have you considered this before? Do you agree?

Chapter 22: Hashtag Friendship

1. What are your motivations for using social media? Are you more concerned with yourself or with others?

2. What are you saying about yourself by what you post on social media? Are you hindering or helping your friendships?

3. How can you be more purposeful with hashtag friendship to enhance real-life relationships?

4. Most importantly, do the externals of your life and how you present yourself online match what's happening internally?

Part 5: Receiving Friendship

Chapter 23: SOS

1. Do you struggle with asking for physical or logistical help from friends? Why or why not?

2. What about asking for emotional or spiritual help? Why is this often more difficult for us?

3. Do you enjoy meeting the needs of your friends? Why, then, do we often believe we are burdens to our friends?

4. Is there something you need help with? Do you need to bring your friends in?

Chapter 24: Heed

1. How do you typically respond when a friend brings something to your attention you don't necessarily want to hear?

2. How can we distinguish whether wounds are from a faithful friend or are motivated by something other than love?

3. What is a wise response to wounding?

4. How is suffering a part of Christian friendship?

Chapter 25: Savor

1. What would life be like without the gift of friendship?

2. Do you focus more on what you lack in friendship or more on what you have? How can you cultivate a thankful heart regarding the women in your life?

3. Think about the women God has placed in your life. How have they been a blessing to you? Thank God for them now. Consider ways to tell them why you're thankful for them.

Lessons on Friendship

When we were young, friendship happened to us. Believing that friendship will "just happen to us" is an immature perspective on adult friendship.

The wish-dream of friendship is a hindrance to real, biblical friendship. When we hold an ideal of friendship in our minds, believing it's attainable, we hold a standard above the heads of the real women God has placed in our lives and then wonder why we're constantly disappointed by the realities, complexities, and difficulties in our relationships.

People are not fillers for a present God, and God is not a placeholder for future friends. The goal of biblical friendship is to secure ourselves to the sure, steadfast anchor of Christ and, while holding to that anchor, give and receive the gift of friendship in a way that brings him glory.

True friendship is not easy. In order to have healthy, biblical friendships, we must be willing to embrace the difficulty and accept that it is for our sanctification.

Our fears are threats to friendship. Friendship will sometimes hurt, but when we willingly work through conflict, knowing we are secure in the love of Christ, instead of deepening fear we will have deepening friendship.

Our insecurities and the assumptions we make about other women are threats to friendship. When we compare ourselves with others, we often think of them according to their secondary identities. These thoughts lead to actions that wound.

Self-preoccupation and entitlement are hindrances to friendship. We must be initiative-takers who seek out other women.

In order to discover and deepen friendships, we have to take the risk of being vulnerable with one another. Vulnerability is the spark of friendship.

In order to discover and deepen friendships, we have to be willing to push through our discomfort and initiate with others.

Inviting other women into our personal spaces is a resource we have to invite deeper friendship.

When we share our stories of redemption, they become God-shaped tools for forging friendship.

In order to discover and deepen friendships, we must make the necessary sacrifices of time, effort, and energy.

If we are women who enter a room thinking *There you are!* rather than *Here I am!* we quickly become influential friend magnets. We can't be friends with everyone but we can use this influence to honor other women and connect them with one another.

Naming our friends is a form of remembering, a marker for stewarding well the friendships God is giving us.

Learning to ask well-placed questions and listening carefully to another's thoughts and emotions are skills that help us know others deeply.

Words are the essence of a friendship. We must be careful to use them well.

God gives us friendship for times of adversity. It is a joy to enter into a friend's difficulty and minister to her.

We are not the Christ. We cannot always fix things for our friends. But we can always pray for them.

Other people don't have the capacity God does, so we shouldn't expect God-like capacity from them.

A faithful friend is one who loves enough to tell the truth and does so carefully.

The primary avenue we have for representing God to people who don't know him, people who don't know anything about our true home, is through friendship.

We want to use our online presence to encourage, champion, thank, and connect with our real-life friends.

In order to receive and deepen friendships, we must learn to ask for help from our friends.

We are wise to listen when friends bring faithful wounds.

Intentionally receive friends as gifts from God. Savor them and thank God for them.

Friends really are friends forever if the Lord is the Lord of them.

Wisdom from the Bible on Friendship

Thus the LORD used to speak to Moses face to face, as a man speaks to his friend.

Exodus 33:11 ESV

If your very own brother, or your son or daughter, or the wife you love, or your closest friend secretly entices you, saying, "Let us go and worship other gods" (gods that neither you nor your ancestors have known, gods of the peoples around you, whether near or far, from one end of the land to the other), do not yield to them or listen to them.

Deuteronomy 13:6–8 NIV

Now when Job's three friends heard of all this evil that had come upon him, they came each from his own place, Eliphaz the Temanite, Bildad the Shuhite, and Zophar the Naamathite. They made an appointment together to come to show him sympathy and comfort him.

Job 2:11 ESV

The friendship of the Lord is for those who fear him, and he makes known to them his covenant.

Psalm 25:14 ESV

My son, if sinners entice you, do not consent.

Proverbs 1:10 ESV

Do not withhold good from those to whom it is due, when it is in your power to do it. Do not say to your neighbor, "Go, and come again, tomorrow I will give it"—when you have it with you. Do not plan evil against your neighbor, who dwells trustingly beside you. Do not contend with a man for no reason, when he has done you no harm.

Proverbs 3:27–30 ESV

[The Lord hates] one who sows discord among brethren.

Proverbs 6:19

Say to wisdom, "You are my sister," and call insight your intimate friend.

Proverbs 7:4 ESV

The wise of heart will receive commandments, but a babbling fool will come to ruin.

Proverbs 10:8 ESV

The mouth of the righteous is a fountain of life, but the mouth of the wicked conceals violence.

Proverbs 10:11 ESV

Hatred stirs up strife, but love covers all offenses.

Proverbs 10:12 ESV

The lips of the righteous feed many.
Proverbs 10:21 ESV

When it goes well with the righteous, the city rejoices.
Proverbs 11:10 ESV

Whoever belittles his neighbor lacks sense, but a man of understanding remains silent.
Proverbs 11:12 ESV

Whoever goes about slandering reveals secrets, but he who is trustworthy in spirit keeps a thing covered.
Proverbs 11:13 ESV

In an abundance of counselors there is safety.
Proverbs 11:14 ESV

The merciful man does good for his own soul.
Proverbs 11:17

Whoever brings blessing will be enriched, and one who waters will himself be watered.
Proverbs 11:25 ESV

Whoever diligently seeks good seeks favor.
Proverbs 11:27 ESV

The righteous should choose his friends carefully.
Proverbs 12:26

Good understanding gains favor, but the way of the unfaithful is hard.

Proverbs 13:15

Poverty and disgrace come to him who ignores instruction, but whoever heeds reproof is honored.

Proverbs 13:18 ESV

Whoever walks with the wise becomes wise, but the companion of fools will suffer harm.

Proverbs 13:20 ESV

Each heart knows its own bitterness, and no one else can share its joy.

Proverbs 14:10 NIV

A soft answer turns away wrath, but a harsh word stirs up anger. The tongue of the wise commends knowledge, but the mouths of fools pour out folly.

Proverbs 15:1–2 ESV

The cheerful of heart has a continual feast.

Proverbs 15:15 ESV

Better is a dinner of herbs where love is than a fattened ox and hatred with it.

Proverbs 15:17 ESV

To make an apt answer is a joy to a man, and a word in season, how good it is!

Proverbs 15:23 ESV

He who is greedy for gain troubles his own house.

Proverbs 15:27

The ear that listens to life-giving reproof will dwell among the wise.

Proverbs 15:31 ESV

When a man's ways please the LORD, he makes even his enemies to be at peace with him.

Proverbs 16:7 ESV

Gracious words are like a honeycomb, sweetness to the soul and health to the body.

Proverbs 16:24 ESV

A dishonest man spreads strife, and a whisperer separates close friends.

Proverbs 16:28 ESV

Whoever covers an offense seeks love, but he who repeats a matter separates close friends.

Proverbs 17:9 ESV

A friend loves at all times, and a brother is born for adversity.

Proverbs 17:17 ESV

Whoever restrains his words has knowledge, and he who has a cool spirit is a man of understanding.

Proverbs 17:27 ESV

Whoever isolates himself seeks his own desire; he breaks out against all sound judgment.

Proverbs 18:1 ESV

A fool takes no pleasure in understanding, but only in expressing his opinion.

Proverbs 18:2 ESV

It is an honor for a man to keep aloof from strife, but every fool will be quarreling.

Proverbs 20:3 ESV

Whoever has a bountiful eye will be blessed, for he shares his bread with the poor.

Proverbs 22:9 ESV

Do not make friends with a hot-tempered person, do not associate with one easily angered, or you may learn their ways and get yourself ensnared.

Proverbs 22:24–25 NIV

Let not your heart envy sinners, but continue in the fear of the Lord all the day. Surely there is a future, and your hope will not be cut off.

Proverbs 23:17–18 ESV

Let your foot be seldom in your neighbor's house, lest he have his fill of you and hate you.

Proverbs 25:17 ESV

Confidence in an unfaithful man in time of trouble is like a bad tooth and a foot out of joint.

Proverbs 25:19

Better is open rebuke than hidden love.

Proverbs 27:5 ESV

Faithful are the wounds of a friend.

Proverbs 27:6 ESV

Ointment and perfume delight the heart, and the sweetness of a man's friend gives delight by hearty counsel.

Proverbs 27:9

Whoever blesses his neighbor with a loud voice, rising early in the morning, will be counted as cursing.

Proverbs 27:14 ESV

Iron sharpens iron, and one man sharpens another.

Proverbs 27:17 ESV

Two are better than one, because they have a good return for their labor: If either of them falls down, one can help the other up. But pity anyone who falls and has no one to help them up.

Ecclesiastes 4:9–10 NIV

So in everything, do to others what you would have them do to you, for this sums up the Law and the Prophets.

Matthew 7:12 NIV

The Son of Man came eating and drinking, and they say, "Look at him! A glutton and a drunkard, a friend of tax collectors and sinners!" Yet wisdom is justified by her deeds.

Matthew 11:19 ESV

As he was getting into the boat, the man who had been possessed with demons begged him that he might be with him. And he did not permit him but said to him, "Go home to your friends and tell them how much the Lord has done for you, and how he has had mercy on you."

Mark 5:18–19 ESV

John answered and said, "A man can receive nothing unless it has been given to him from heaven. You yourselves bear me witness, that I said, 'I am not the Christ,' but, 'I have been sent before Him.' He who has the bride is the bridegroom; but the friend of the bridegroom, who stands and hears him, rejoices greatly because of the bridegroom's voice. Therefore this joy of mine is fulfilled. He must increase, but I must decrease."

John 3:27–30

Greater love has no one than this, that someone lay down his life for his friends. You are my friends if you do what I command you. No longer do I call you servants, for the servant does not know what his master is doing; but I have called you friends, for all that I have heard from my Father I have made known to you.

John 15:13–15 ESV

They devoted themselves to the apostles' teaching and to fellowship, to the breaking of bread and to prayer.

Acts 2:42 NIV

In everything I did, I showed you that by this kind of hard work we must help the weak, remembering the words the Lord Jesus himself said: "It is more blessed to give than to receive."

Acts 20:35 NIV

God is faithful, who has called you into fellowship with his Son, Jesus Christ our Lord.

1 Corinthians 1:9 NIV

Blessed be the God and Father of our Lord Jesus Christ, the Father of mercies and God of all comfort, who comforts us in all our tribulation, that we may be able to comfort those who are in any trouble, with the comfort with which we ourselves are comforted by God.

2 Corinthians 1:3–4

Therefore, from now on, we regard no one according to the flesh. Even though we have known Christ according to the flesh, yet now we know Him thus no longer. Therefore, if anyone is in Christ, he is a new creation; old things have passed away; behold, all things have become new.

2 Corinthians 5:16–17

Bear one another's burdens, and so fulfill the law of Christ.

Galatians 6:2

Be completely humble and gentle; be patient, bearing with one another in love.

Ephesians 4:2 NIV

So if there is any encouragement in Christ, any comfort from love, any participation in the Spirit, any affection and sympathy, complete my joy by being of the same mind, having the same love, being in full accord and of one mind. Do nothing from selfish ambition or conceit, but in humility count others more significant than yourselves. Let each of you look not only to his own interests, but also to the interests of others.

Philippians 2:1–4 ESV

Therefore, as the elect of God, holy and beloved, put on tender mercies, kindness, humility, meekness, longsuffering; bearing with one another, and forgiving one another, if anyone has a complaint against another; even as Christ forgave you, so you also must do. But above all these things put on love, which is the bond of perfection. And let the peace of God rule in your hearts, to which also you were called in one body; and be thankful.

Colossians 3:12–15

In everything give thanks; for this is the will of God in Christ Jesus for you.

1 Thessalonians 5:18

And let us consider one another in order to stir up love and good works.

Hebrews 10:24

My dear brothers and sisters, take note of this: Everyone should be quick to listen, slow to speak and slow to become angry.

James 1:19 NIV

Where do wars and fights come from among you? Do they not come from your desires for pleasure that war in your members?

James 4:1

You adulterous people! Do you not know that friendship with the world is enmity with God? Therefore whoever wishes to be a friend of the world makes himself an enemy of God.

James 4:4 ESV

Live such good lives among the pagans that, though they accuse you of doing wrong, they may see your good deeds and glorify God on the day he visits us.

1 Peter 2:12 NIV

Be hospitable to one another without grumbling. As each one has received a gift, minister it to one another, as good stewards of the manifold grace of God.

1 Peter 4:9–10

This is the message we have heard from him and proclaim to you, that God is light, and in him is no darkness at all. If we say we have fellowship with him while we walk in darkness, we lie and do not practice the truth. But if we walk in the light, as he is in the light, we have fellowship with one another, and the blood of Jesus his Son cleanses us from all sin.

1 John 1:5–7 ESV

We love because he first loved us.
1 John 4:19 ESV

Notes

Chapter 1 When Did Friendship Become Such a Struggle?

1. Dietrich Bonhoeffer, *Life Together* (New York: Harper & Row, 1954), 17.

Chapter 2 The Dreams We Have for Friendship

1. Bonhoeffer, *Life Together*, 30.
2. Jonathan Cain, "Faithfully," on Journey, *Frontiers*, Sony/ATV Music, 1983.
3. Bonhoeffer, *Life Together*, 26.
4. Ibid.
5. Ibid., 27–28.

Chapter 3 How God Gives Friendship

1. Exodus 33:11; 2 Chronicles 20:7.
2. James 4:4.
3. Joseph Scriven, "What a Friend We Have in Jesus," public domain, 1855.
4. 1 John 1:3.
5. 1 John 1:7.
6. 1 Corinthians 1:9; Philippians 1:5.
7. Augustine of Hippo, *Confessions*, 3.6.11.
8. Bonhoeffer, *Life Together*, 20.

Chapter 4 Messy Beautiful Friendship

1. Bonhoeffer, *Life Together*, 28–29.
2. Proverbs 27:17.

Chapter 5 Fear of Being Burned

1. C. S. Lewis, *The Four Loves* (New York: Harcourt Brace, 1960), 72.
2. John 16:33 NIV.
3. Ibid.

Chapter 6 Ashes of Insecurity

1. Jonathan Holmes, *The Company We Keep: In Search of Biblical Friendship* (Cruciform Press, 2014), Kindle ed.
2. C. S. Lewis, *The Weight of Glory* (New York: Macmillan, 1949), 151.

Chapter 7 Kindling for the Campfire

1. Hugh Black, *Friendship* (New York: Fleming H. Revell, 1898), 40.
2. Lewis, *Four Loves*, 66–67.

Chapter 12 Dance Card

1. Tim Keller, "Friendship," sermon recording, May 29, 2005, accessed December 3, 2015, http://www.gospelinlife.com/friendship-5396.
2. Cassie Brand, "My Card Is Full: The Evolution of the Farewell Ball Dance Cards," *Archive Journal* no. 2 (2012), http://www.archivejournal.net/issue/2/archives-remixed/my-card-is-full/.

Chapter 19 Room to Breathe

1. Bonhoeffer, *Life Together*, 35–36.

Chapter 20 Faithful Wounds

1. Tim Keller, Twitter post, @timkellernyc, December 29, 2015, https://twitter.com/timkellernyc/status/681852634698006528.

Chapter 21 Homesick

1. Lewis, *Weight of Glory*, 30–31.
2. Oswald Chambers, *My Utmost for His Highest* (Uhrichsville, OH: Barbour, 1935), June 10.

Chapter 23 SOS

1. Bonhoeffer, *Life Together*, 22–23.

Chapter 25 Savor

1. Ralph Waldo Emerson, "Friendship," *Essays: First Series* (1841), accessed February 20, 2016, http://www.emersoncentral.com/friendship.htm.
2. Bonhoeffer, *Life Together*, 28–29.
3. Lewis, *Four Loves*, 89–90.

Conclusion

1. Lewis, *Four Loves*, 89–90.
2. Michael W. Smith, "Friends," *Change Your World*, Reunion Records, 1992.
3. Keller, "Friendship."

About the Author

Christine Hoover is a pastor's wife and a mom of three boys. She is the author of *The Church Planting Wife* and *From Good to Grace*, and her work has appeared on *Desiring God*, *The Gospel Coalition*, *(in)courage*, and *For The Church*. Through her blog, *Grace Covers Me*, she enjoys helping women apply the gift of God's grace to their daily lives. She lives in Virginia.

Connect with Christine:
www.GraceCoversMe.com
Twitter: @christinehoover
Instagram: @christinehoover98

Also Available from
Christine Hoover

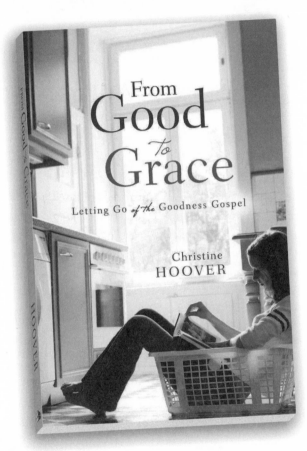

We can find ourselves living by a lesser gospel: the gospel of goodness. It's a gospel without grace, and in the end it's good for nothing. But God is calling us to something greater than good. Rather than serving God out of obligation or duty, be compelled to love and serve God with great joy.

Follow Author

CHRISTINE HOOVER

· ·

Blog: gracecoversme.com

f facebook.com/GraceCoversMe

🐦 @ChristineHoover

📷 @ChristineHoover98

LIKE THIS
BOOK?

Consider sharing it with others!

- Share or mention the book on your social media platforms. Use the hashtag **#MessyBeautifulFriendship**.

- Write a book review on your blog or on a retailer site.

- Pick up a copy for friends, family, or strangers—anyone who you think would enjoy and be challenged by its message!

- Share this message on Twitter or Facebook: **I loved #MessyBeautifulFriendship by @ChristineHoover // GraceCoversMe.com @ReadBakerBooks**

- Recommend this book for your church, workplace, book club, or class.

- Follow Baker Books on social media and tell us what you like.

 Facebook.com/ReadBakerBooks

 @ReadBakerBooks